"*Soul Care* is a wise and helpful resource for experiencing the interconnected restoration of body, mind, and spirit that so often feels just out of reach. It's a hopeful invitation to more fully realize the beautiful kingdom of God vision for human flourishing together."

—**Katherine Wolf**, author of *Treasures in the Dark, Suffer Strong*, and *Hope Heals*

"This book is such a gift for the days in which we are living. We are pulled in so many directions, often stretched almost to the breaking point. Debra guides us to places of rest and peace and joy with a profound understanding of the Word of God and the human soul."

—**Sheila Walsh**, author and TV host

"As a professional counselor, Debra possesses a unique vantage point on this critical topic. I've seen too many Christians burn out because they wanted to proclaim the message of Jesus without emulating the pace of Jesus. I'm praying this resource will help a multitude of saints endure for years to come because they follow our Savior's rhythms of rest and war."

—**Ben Stuart**, pastor of Passion City Church DC; author of *Single, Dating, Engaged, Married* and *Rest & War*

"If you often find yourself feeling depleted—whether from selflessly caring for others at your own expense or from simply not realizing there's another way—*Soul Care* invit⋯ ⋯⋯ ⋯⋯ a beautiful journey of refreshment and refilling. This book ⋯⋯ ⋯t God's plan for you includes not jus⋯ ⋯⋯ s wealth of wisdom and experience ⋯⋯ ⋯r rediscovering the vibrant life God e⋯

—**Jennie Lusko**, author and p⋯⋯ ⋯st

SOUL

+

CARE

SOUL + CARE

DEBRA FILETA
M.A., LPC

HARVEST HOUSE PUBLISHERS
EUGENE, OREGON

Scripture versions used can be found in the back of this book.

Cover design by Faceout Studio, Spencer Fuller

Interior design by Angie Renich, Wildwood Digital Publishing

For bulk, special sales, or ministry purchases, please call 1-800-547-8979.
Email: CustomerService@hhpbooks.com

This logo is a federally registered trademark of the Hawkins Children's LLC.
Harvest House Publishers, Inc., is the exclusive licensee of this trademark.

Soul Care
Copyright © 2024 by Debra Fileta
Published by Harvest House Publishers
Eugene, Oregon 97408

www.harvesthousepublishers.cm

ISBN 978-0-7369-8821-6 (pbk.)
ISBN 978-0-7369-8822-3 (eBook)
ISBN 978-0-7369-9149-0 (Audio)

Library of Congress Control Number: 2024931183

Printed in the United States of America

24 25 26 27 28 29 30 31 32 / BP / 10 9 8 7 6 5 4 3 2 1

To my first-born child, Elisabeth "Ella" Fileta.
You are wise beyond your 13 years. I am so grateful for your servant heart, your helping spirit, and your deep desire to please God. My prayer for you is that you would learn to always stay "filled up" so that you can continue to pour out in the way that God has called you to. Don't ever let that get out of balance. I'm so proud of you and honored to be your mom.

Contents

Foreword

by Tim Timberlake

AMID THE FRENETIC PACE OF OUR MODERN WORLD, where hustle and grind often feel like badges of honor, the concept of "soul care" may seem foreign, even impractical. But as you hold this book in your hands and prepare to embark on a journey toward more profound understanding and practice, I implore you to pause for a moment. Take a deep breath. Reflect on your own life and the moments when you felt most alive, most connected, and most at peace. Chances are that those moments had something to do with your soul's well-being.

Soul Care isn't just another self-help book. It's a lifeline, an invitation to rediscover the rhythms that make you whole and connected to your most authentic self. It's a call to embrace the wisdom of the ages and integrate it into your modern, fast-paced life. It explores the delicate balance between the spiritual and the physical, the profound and the practical, and the eternal and the everyday.

Through a journey of personal discovery and transformation, Debra realized a fundamental truth: In the pursuit of spiritual growth and resilience, we often overlook the importance of taking care of our physical bodies. This subtle yet profound revelation can reshape how you view your well-being. It's the understanding that sometimes, the answer to your struggles and suffering might be as simple as drinking more water. But it's also more than that; it's about recognizing your role and responsibility in your journey toward wholeness.

The Bible is a source of timeless wisdom, and in its pages, water is not just a metaphor but a tangible symbol of life, cleansing, and sustenance. It's a testament to the idea that soul care is holistic, encompassing both the spiritual and the physical. From the Old Testament to the New, water flows through the Scriptures as a reminder of God's provision and care. Just as God provided for the Israelites in the desert, He offers the same to us. Water represents life, salvation, and the Word of God itself.

In Jesus's humanity, we find a profound lesson. When He, fully God and fully man, uttered the simple words "I thirst" as He hung on the cross, it was an acknowledgment of His humanity, a reminder that even amid profound spiritual purpose, He had physical needs. His request for a drink was a call for refreshment, not just for His body, but for His soul. In His final moments, He revealed the intimate connection between physical well-being and spiritual fulfillment.

This book will guide you toward rediscovering your life-giving rhythms, reminding you that caring for your soul is not a luxury but a necessity. This journey involves acknowledging your physical needs, tending to your spiritual health, and understanding that the two are intricately intertwined.

As you delve into the pages of this book, I encourage you to approach it with an open heart and a willingness to embrace the practical and spiritual dimensions of soul care. The insights you'll find here are not just theoretical but deeply practical, designed to help you find rest during life's chaos, avoid burnout, and experience unshakable joy.

In a world that often emphasizes "more" and "faster," this book invites you to consider the counterintuitive power of "less" and "slower." It's a call to reconnect with your true self, embrace the rhythms that nurture your soul, and ultimately experience the peace and fulfillment that come from aligning your physical and spiritual well-being.

May the wisdom contained within these pages be a wellspring of inspiration and transformation as you embark on your own soul-care journey. And, like Jesus at the well, may you find not only refreshment for your body but also nourishment for your soul.

Pastor Tim Timberlake
Senior Pastor, Celebration Church
Author, *The Art of Overcoming* and *The Power of 1440*

SOUL CARE

Living Filled to Fully Live

Chapter 1

FUEL UP

How Full Do You Feel?

I'M ABOUT TO ASK YOU A REALLY IMPORTANT QUESTION.
I know, I know, we just got past the title of the book. We barely know each other yet, we don't even know what this book is about or where exactly it's going, and here I am, about to throw a deep question your way. I didn't even bother to write an introduction to ease you into it. We're just diving into the emotional deep end, aren't we? I'll blame it on the counselor side of me. But here's the thing: The answer to this question will set the stage for the rest of this book. The answer to this question is what places you in either the category of people who are thriving or people who are surviving. The answer to this question will help me predict what type of person you are and what your life will look like one year from today. So, like I said, it's a really important question.

The question is this: How full do you feel right now?

I don't mean physically full, as in you just scarfed down a sandwich or a salad for lunch and you're feeling uncomfortable because you ate too fast.

I mean *emotionally* full. What I'm really talking about is the fullness of purpose, energy, motivation, peace, joy, creativity, strength, hope, and connection. Maybe it will be easier for you to answer my question when you think about the opposite end of the spectrum. The opposite of fullness is emptiness. Emptiness means overwhelm, lack of motivation, low energy, fatigue, depression or anxiety, loneliness, hopelessness, apathy, tiredness, cynicism, and general burnout.

How full do you feel right now? Or maybe I should ask, how empty?

If I asked you to tell me on a scale of zero to ten (ten being *extremely full* and zero being *completely empty*) what number would you give yourself?

Think about that for a moment.

Don't answer right away.

In fact, put this book down for a moment and really think about your answer before you move on. Pause for a moment and tune out what might be going on around you, then try to tune in to what's going on inside of you. Because that's exactly what it's going to take to get an accurate answer to my question: the ability to tune out the external noise and tune in to what your body is telling you.

FUELING STYLES

As a professional counselor, I'm often challenging and encouraging people to tune in to how they're feeling—but I would love it if somehow we could figure out how to get some of these answers in an easier, more objective way. Wouldn't it be nice if we had some sort of meter on our bodies that allowed us to accurately see how full we are feeling, like the gas tank gauge on a car? Imagine if we could see that little needle, starting at *F* when we're full, and slowly making its way down toward *E* as we're nearing empty? I guarantee you I'd have far fewer clients coming into my counseling office in a state of complete crisis and total burnout if that feature existed on the human body. We could just track our fullness as we went through life, stopping to fill up as soon as the needle started ticking below the quarter-tank mark on our emotional reservoir.

For a quick moment, let me detour from this conversation and acknowledge that some of you out there are utterly shocked right now that

I suggested filling up at the quarter-tank mark. Because when it comes to your "gas fueling styles," you're less like me and more like my husband: the type of person who likes to live on the edge when it comes to filling up your gas tank. You like to let that gas gauge get as close to *E* as possible before you fill up. You get some strange sort of satisfaction—a satisfaction that people like me will never understand—from seeing that gas gauge light up, warning that you have less than 20 miles left before Empty. (I would say *sick* satisfaction, but I don't want to offend anyone quite so early on in the book.) You're the type of person who coasts into the gas station on nothing but fumes, stopping to fill up only when you absolutely have to and not a moment before. Listen, I see you.

The truth of the matter is, I don't know if our gas fueling styles have anything to do with our *emotional* filling styles, and I don't know whether you're a quarter-tank kind of person, like me, or a live-on-the-edge-until-I-hit-*E* kind of person like my husband. But no matter what kind of person you are, we all have an emotional tank that needs filling. We all have an emotional capacity that we need to be acutely aware of in order to avoid burnout, depression, anxiety, and significant emotional crisis. We all have a responsibility to stay filled in order to live a peace-filled, thriving, joyful life.

Jesus called it living a *full* life (John 10:10).

LIVING FILLED

The contrast to living filled is living empty—and living empty is the exact way the enemy wants us to live. In contrast to the way of Jesus, which is to live fully and abundantly, John 10:10 tell us that "the thief comes only to steal and kill and destroy." God's Word is referring to Satan, our enemy, the thief who wants to empty out our lives completely and steal all our resources, time, energy, motivation, purpose, and joy. He wants to rob us and drain every ounce of our emotional and spiritual reservoir so we're either unable or unwilling to live the full lives God calls us to live.

We are ineffective when we are completely empty because our level of impact has a direct correlation with our level of fullness. We cannot love and serve others well out of a place of emptiness, which is exactly why the enemy wants to sieve every last drop out of our lives. But God's will is for us to live filled. Because we can't live fully until we live filled. If the enemy wants to steal, kill, and destroy, Jesus wants to fill us, restore us, and renew us. Take a look at the contrast in John 10:10 and see Jesus's desire for our lives in a few different translations:

"I have come that they may have life, and have it to the full" (NIV).

"My purpose is to give them a rich and satisfying life" (NLT).

"I came that they may have life, and have it abundantly" (ESV).

"I came so everyone would have life, and have it fully" (CEV).

"I have come in order that you might have life—life in all its fullness (GNT).

Life *in all its fullness.* Doesn't that sound so good?

Why is it, then, that so many people aren't feeling full? Why are so many Christians I interact with on a regular basis feeling the exact opposite of full? Why are most of the people I meet with in my counseling office—and many of the people I connect with as I travel the country on speaking trips—good, spiritual, God-loving people, yet their lives are marked by burnout, depletion, emptiness, stress, and busyness? They're living on *E.*

> Our level of impact has a direct correlation with our level of fullness.

We must be doing something wrong.

Maybe in our best attempts at serving God, loving others, caring for our families, and winning souls for Jesus, we've actually forgotten what it means to check in with our own level of fullness—to get a healthy measure of how we're doing spiritually and emotionally, to stop and take the time to nourish and nurture our own souls. Maybe while we've been distracted with our full schedules and our to-do lists, our many goals and agendas, our important ministries, and our meetings, we've allowed ourselves to slowly tick toward *E* without noticing. We've come to live in a place of emptiness rather than a place of fullness. Or maybe, just maybe, we've never actually learned *how* to fill up. We've never learned how to truly care for our souls.

Some of my biggest inspirations for this book, and specifically for the upcoming sections of this book, are the life and rhythms of Jesus. As I studied the Gospels in preparation for my time of writing, one thing that stood out to me was the fact that Jesus, though He was fully God, was also fully man. He understood the limitations of His human body. He was acutely aware of the fact that His body had a capacity. And He was so intentional about staying filled so He could pour out for the people God had called Him to fill up. What if we could live with this type of awareness? What if we could honor our own capacity, learn to fill up and stay filled, long before we reached the point of empty?

Over the next few chapters of this book, we're going on a journey of filling up. We'll not only assess our level of fullness, but we'll also keep track of our level of emptiness. We'll learn the purpose and meaning and value of caring for our souls, and then we'll discover exactly how to do it in six different categories: Nourish, Rest, Connect, Protect, Savor, and Tune In. It's a six-part process that I like to call *Soul Care.*

> Empty people can't pour out because they have nothing left to give.

Step-by-step, I'm going to help you discover some of the most important rhythms that I have been inspired by and learned so much from, all through the life of Jesus—rhythms I not only apply in my own life but also teach my clients, as well as the thousands of church members, pastors, and leaders I have the privilege of serving and teaching across the country.

Empty people can't pour out because they have nothing left to give. That's why we're going on a journey of filling up, so we can keep pouring effectively and indefinitely into those whom God has called us to pour into: our spouses, our children, our families, our friends, our churches, our communities, and our ministries.

I don't know how you answered my initial question above—How full do you feel right now?—but I hope you have an answer by now. And whether your answer is a zero or a ten, a four or a six, or somewhere in between—no matter what level of fullness or emptiness you're feeling today—it's time to take seriously the importance of fueling up. It's time to take seriously the call of living life in all its fullness. I'm so ready and excited and privileged to help you get there. If you're ready, too, let's do it together.

Verse for Reflection

The thief comes only to steal and kill and destroy;
I have come that they may have life, and have it to the full (John 10:10).

Today's Rhythm: HOW FULL DO YOU FEEL?

1. How full do you feel in this season of your life (zero being "I feel completely empty," ten being "I feel extremely full")?

2. List out some of the things that tend to drain you of your energy, motivation, and joy.

3. In contrast, list out some of the things that tend to fill you up and give you energy, motivation, and joy.

4. Think of a time when you felt like you were "living on empty." What was going on in that season? What were some of the signs and symptoms you were on E? In what ways did the emptiness impact your life and the lives of those around you?

Chapter 2

SELF-CARE VERSUS SOUL CARE

Assess Your Beliefs

I MENTIONED EARLIER THAT I DIDN'T WANT TO OFFEND anyone on the first page. But here we are at page 23, and I'm starting to feel a little more comfortable with you. So, I'm just going to say it. Christians tend to be really bad at caring for themselves. I know, it's a sweeping statement, but I've noticed a significant trend in the clients I work with who are struggling with burnout: Deep down, they believe that caring for themselves is somehow wrong—or even anti-biblical. And here is why this matters: The signs of burnout are symptoms of a much deeper belief system that's going on underneath the surface—a belief system that is preventing or inhibiting us from caring for ourselves.

And it's no wonder that Christians struggle with this more than the average person. We're often taught to believe that caring for others automatically means *not* caring for ourselves. Scripture makes it clear that we aren't to value ourselves above others, because we are *all* valuable because of Jesus (Philippians 2:3). God's Word is also very clear that we shouldn't *only* think of ourselves and our own needs (Philippians 2:4). But nowhere in Scripture are we encouraged to neglect or abuse ourselves. Nowhere

in Scripture are we told to ignore our needs and the state of our personal health. Yet that is exactly what we're doing when we reach a point of burnout. We are neglecting and abusing ourselves, somehow convinced that by doing so, we're doing God's work. By taking Scripture out of context, we continue in a cycle of pain, sin, and struggle. Like I said before, we can't care for others well when we ourselves are depleted, unhealthy, and burned-out. Because no matter how much we wish we could, empty people can't fill others up.

> Caring for ourselves is an act of honoring the temples God has given us!

I also recognize that for many of us, the reason we struggle to truly believe in the value of caring for ourselves is because we associate it with the concept of self-care. I've been in the church long enough to acknowledge that *self-care* is a loaded term for so many people. When was the last time you heard a Sunday sermon about the concept of self-care (besides hearing me speak)?

"Self-care isn't biblical," said one popular Christian author in a random podcast interview I happened to hear. "Self-care is demonic," is a phrase a credible pastor I know confessed that he used to say and actually used to believe (*used to* being the key words). There's been a general sense of animosity toward the concept of self-care among spiritual leaders. And if I'm honest, it was surprising for me to hear these things. Coming from the world of counseling and emotional health, I've always believed that the concept of self-care, or caring for ourselves, is an act of honoring the temples God has given us! "Don't you realize that your body is the temple of the Holy Spirit, who lives in you and was given to you by God? You do not belong to yourself" (1 Corinthians 6:19 NLT). If anything, that verse reminds me of the responsibility, privilege, and honor it is to care for myself. My body is not my own; it belongs to an Almighty God. I need to learn to treat my entire body—mentally, emotionally, spiritually, and physically—with the respect, honor, and value it deserves.

THE SELF IN SELF-CARE

As I've tried to understand the negative feelings toward the idea of self-care, it seems to be rooted in the fact that the phrase is centered on the word *self*. Some Christians seem afraid that if we focus too much on self, we'll become self-absorbed. So their response is to do the opposite, which is to *never* focus on the self. In other words, self-neglect. I don't know about you, but both of those words have the word *self* in them, and the temptation for self to be the one and only focus still exists on either side of the equation. Whether we're self-absorbed or self-neglecting, we will end up becoming the center of our worlds. Because, ironically, when you are burned-out, depleted, and depressed, the only thing you think about is yourself. Your pain and struggles become the focus of your life.

I'm reminded of the phrase, "Humility is not thinking less of yourself; it is thinking of yourself less."[1] This isn't about self-neglect, or making ourselves out to be unimportant, unvaluable, and unworthy—it's about caring for ourselves so we are so healthy and filled up enough to overflow into the lives of everyone around us. A healthy person has the bandwidth and the resources to meet the needs of others. A healthy person has the ability to care for others in the way that God has called them to.

DEEPER THAN SELF-CARE

Though I'm a fan of the concept of self-care, and though I do not believe that self-care is an anti-Christian phrase, I want us to go much deeper than self-care throughout the pages of this book. When people talk about self-care in the context of our modern society and culture, they're typically referring to things that make us feel good: taking a hot bath, getting a mani-pedi, or going on a tropical vacation. When people refer to self-care in the context of the field of counseling and psychology, they're typically referring to healthy rituals that fill you up throughout your day.

Things like going for a walk, listening to music, getting a massage, reading a good book, engaging in a hobby or interest, etc. And while I believe in the importance, value, and fun in *all of the above*—both in the way culture defines it as well as the way the world of psychology defines it—I want us to take this concept even deeper.

> A healthy person has the ability to care for others in the way that God has called them to.

I want us to start seeing it in terms of soul care: rhythms and practices that fuel and feed and strengthen our souls—the deepest parts of who we are. Routines that help us become the best versions of ourselves emotionally, mentally, physically, and spiritually.

Over the next few chapters, we're going to take a closer look at the concept of soul care and how to apply it to our lives. But we can't really start there, because first, we must get to the bottom of *what* you actually believe about the concept of caring for yourself—and *why*. You must come to terms with the fact that your level of fullness is ultimately attached to your underlying beliefs and understanding of the importance of caring for your soul. Maybe you've lived your life trying not to be selfish, self-focused, or self-absorbed, but in the end you've found yourself self-neglecting, self-sabotaging, and self-destructing. I don't want that to be your story.

Your body is not your own. You are not your own. You are a temple of the Holy Spirit. God has entrusted you to care for this temple. What a great honor and privilege. If all of that is true, then soul care cannot just be a luxury; it must be our responsibility. I want you to get ready to search your heart and ask God what it really means to be a person who lives abundantly—a person who is so filled up that they naturally overflow into the lives of those around them. I want that to be my story. And I want it to be yours as well. Let's learn to care for our bodies and to treat them well.

The truth of the matter is that soul care practices don't just matter for the here and now; they also matter for eternity. Because kingdom work is the overflow of an abundant life. Let's learn what it looks like to honor God with all we've got. Starting with ourselves.

Verse for Reflection

Don't you realize that your body is the temple of the Holy Spirit, who lives in you and was given to you by God? You do not belong to yourself (1 Corinthians 6:19 NLT).

Today's Rhythm: ASSESS YOUR BELIEFS

1. What reaction do you have to the concept of self-care? Why? What reaction do you have to the concept of soul care? Why? Where did your beliefs come from? How did your family of origin model—or fail to model—soul care?

2. When it comes to the spectrum of being self-absorbed to self-neglecting, on which side do you tend to find yourself more often? In what ways has this impacted your life and your relationships?

3. Do you consider yourself a temple of the Holy Spirit? In what ways do you honor that temple? In what ways do you tend to neglect that temple?

4. How can caring for yourself have a kingdom impact? How can it have an impact on your marriage, children, family, friends, career, and ministry?

Chapter 3

DON'T PUSH THROUGH

Look for Signals

WHEN I MET JEREMY, HE WAS AT HIS BREAKING POINT.
So much so that he thought he might be having some sort of severe midlife crisis. "I can't do this anymore," he said, fighting back the tears that threatened to choke him up and flood the conversation, holding them back in the way he had always done. "There's so much pulling on me that I feel like I'm going to break." I could hear the overwhelm in his voice and see the pain in his eyes. What made it even more difficult was that this existential crisis was coming at one of the highest points in his life.

He was the pastor of a thriving church on the West Coast, a church he had built from the ground up, a church that was growing faster than he could keep up with. But he felt like he had hit a wall. Not only was he struggling emotionally, feeling a lack of motivation and purpose, but his physical health was also suffering. He was having heart issues and migraines, and even breaking out in hives. The stress had gotten so high that you could literally see it on his body. His heart rate was spiking, and his body felt like it could collapse under the pressure of it all. "I'm overwhelmed, and I'm exhausted. I've been running hard and fast for 15 years, and now I feel like I can't run anymore. I'm done."

Done. Have you ever felt *done*? Totally over it. That feeling of complete and utter depletion, when you knew you just couldn't take another step? I've been there, in different seasons of my life. I remember one of the first times I ever felt this extreme level of fatigue was as a brand-new mom trying to cope with the overwhelming changes of having an infant for the very first time. Not only was I completely sleep-deprived and trying to keep this fussy five-week-old baby girl alive, but I was often managing this new normal alone. As much as he wanted to be right by my side, my husband was a medical resident at the time, working well over 100 hours a week to get through his residency training. Often having to be at the hospital on nights and weekends, he got one weekend off each month (what we called his "golden weekend"). His demanding schedule, plus our sleep deprivation, plus all the physical and hormonal changes I was going through, plus the fact that we had just brought this colicky little baby into the world who cried 12 hours a day, plus the fact that we had no clue what we were doing—it all added up to us both hitting a wall. We each felt *done* in our own way. I remember many nights, tears streaming down my face after putting the baby down to sleep, thanking God that the day had ended exactly when it did because I didn't think I could survive another minute of the exhaustion. I was done. Done. Done. *Done.*

I wish I could tell you that was the last time in my life I ever felt that awful feeling of complete and utter physical and emotional exhaustion. I wish I could tell you it only came with that season of bringing new babies into the world. But I can't. Because burnout can reach us at any given point. It can reach us in the lows of life, just as it can reach us in the highs of life. I'm sure you can relate. We all go through seasons in our lives when we feel like we've reached empty. We're done. We've got nothing left to give. And like my client Jeremy, we feel our bodies crying out for relief.

But one thing I've learned over the years, both in my personal life and in my professional life, is that our bodies are trying to tell us something. They are sending us a message. Burnout is the body's way of crying out for us to *pay attention*. It's the SOS signal from our nervous system telling us to stop and care for ourselves. But rather than see the signs of burnout as a signal to stop and fill up, so many people do the exact opposite. They try to push through. They judge themselves for feeling exhausted, depleted, and low. They hide, and repress, and numb all the hard feelings and *just...keep...going*. But that's like seeing all the emergency lights going off on your car dashboard and assuming they will all go away if you just keep driving. I can tell you from experience: That doesn't work. (You may have read about my lemon of a car in my book *Reset*.) It doesn't work with cars, and it doesn't work in life. When you don't stop to repair, you'll eventually just break down.

LOOK FOR THE SIGNALS

The signs of burnout are important for us to understand because they don't happen overnight. And they don't happen all at once. The signals of burnout pop up here and there. They tend to get more intense and more frequent with time. But if we're aware of the signs and symptoms, we can recognize them and take action before we hit the breaking point. Here are some signs you might be nearing burnout:

- Feeling overwhelmed more often than usual
- More than usual loss of motivation or energy
- Feeling tired, drained, exhausted, or fatigued
- Feeling helpless, trapped, or defeated
- Increased depression or anxiety
- Feeling alone or isolated, even when you're with people
- A nagging sense of failure, self-doubt, or insecurity
- Struggling with a negative or cynical outlook on life
- Feeling apathy, irritability, impatience, bitterness, resentment, or anger toward yourself, God, or others
- An increase in physical symptoms—such as headaches or

migraines, aches and pains, stomach or digestive issues, heart palpitations (skipped beats) or tachycardia (fast heart rate) unrelated to underlying medical issues

- Finding yourself thinking or saying "I can't do this" or "I'm done"
- A lack of enjoyment and excitement in life[1]

> If we're aware of the signs and symptoms, we can recognize them and take action before we hit the breaking point.

Now that you've read through the prior list, ask yourself what signals your body may be sending you. More importantly, how are you responding to those signals? Do you ignore them and keep pushing through? Do you try and tune out the signals by numbing yourself with screens, devices, drugs, alcohol, shopping, porn, food, sugar, entertainment, and busyness? Do you judge yourself with guilt and shame and then try and do even more? Or do you listen and respond to the signals, stop and care for yourself, and bring your body back into alignment?

RESPOND TO THE SIGNALS

I worked closely with Jeremy over the next few months to help him identify the signals his body was sending him, and more importantly, to teach him how to respond to those signals. As we talked through how he ended up here, it quickly became clear that even though it may have felt sudden, getting to his breaking point didn't happen overnight.

The signs and signals had slowly risen to the surface of his life—yet he'd chosen to ignore them and push through. Even as the pastor and spiritual leader of a thriving megachurch, he had never really learned to care for himself, and there were deep reasons why. I'll share more of Jeremy's story with you throughout the pages of this book, as well as other stories along the way, but for now I want to remind you that the good news about burnout is that it doesn't happen overnight. You don't wake up one day feeling utterly empty when you were feeling extremely full the day before. There's a predictable pattern to note—clear signals your body is sending you along the way. But on the flip side, filling up doesn't happen overnight either. There is a process, a learning curve to caring for your soul. And unfortunately, it's one we don't talk about often enough in the church until something, or someone, breaks down.

> God is longing to help us bring our bodies back into alignment by His power and strength.

God is longing to help us bring us our bodies back into alignment by His power and strength.

It's crucial for us to tune in to our bodies and allow our God-given insight to help us recognize the signals. Our bodies are crying out for relief. And it's about time we start to listen and respond.

Verse for Reflection

He gives strength to the weary and increases the power of the weak (Isaiah 40:29).

Today's Rhythm: LOOK FOR SIGNALS

1. Out of the signals of burnout, which are listed again here, check the ones you've experienced in the past three months. List any other signals your body may be revealing to you:

   ☐ Feeling overwhelmed more often than usual

   ☐ More than usual loss of motivation or energy

   ☐ Feeling tired, drained, exhausted, or fatigued

   ☐ Feeling helpless, trapped, or defeated

   ☐ Increased depression or anxiety

   ☐ Feeling alone or isolated, even when you're with people

   ☐ A nagging sense of failure, self-doubt, or insecurity

   ☐ Struggling with a negative or cynical outlook on life

   ☐ Feeling apathy, irritability, impatience, bitterness, resentment, or anger toward yourself, God, or others

   ☐ An increase in physical symptoms—such as headaches or migraines, aches and pains, stomach or digestive issues, heart palpitations (skipped beats) or tachycardia (fast heart rate) unrelated to underlying medical issues

   ☐ Finding yourself thinking or saying "I can't do this" or "I'm done"

   ☐ A lack of enjoyment and excitement in life

2. How do you typically respond to the signals of burnout?

    a. Ignore them and push through the pain

    b. Numb yourself so you don't feel them

    c. Judge yourself or put yourself down

    d. Stop and respond appropriately

3. If you chose a, b, or c, write down why you chose your answer. For example, someone might write: "Here are the ways I numb myself: I tend to rely on shopping and food to block out my uncomfortable feelings and try to make myself feel better. I also tune out at the end of the day by binge-watching Netflix until I fall asleep rather than giving myself time to process what's going on in my life."

4. Write a list of some ways you can stop and respond to your body in this season of life.

Chapter 4

DON'T SELF-DESTRUCT

Confront Your View of Self

"WHY DO I FEEL SO BAD WHEN THERE'S NOTHING SERI-ously wrong with my life?"

This is probably the question I hear most often from people who come into my office struggling with burnout. They don't always know to call it burnout; they just know something feels terribly wrong, even when there's nothing terribly wrong in their life. Jeremy (whom I introduced you to earlier) was struggling with that very question. His life was good. He was happily married with three children who were all healthy. He had a thriving church in a bustling city, and they were making a positive impact on their community. So why did he feel so bad?

I think the answer to this question comes down to one word: *capacity*. Human beings are finite. We have limits, confines, and capabilities. When we exceed our capacity, we start to feel it. It's our body's way of graciously telling us to pay attention and do something different. But why do so many people push through and ignore all the signals we mentioned earlier? Because deep down, a faulty belief system is telling them to keep going anyway. Sometimes that belief system is rooted in a false view of Scripture, as we talked about in a previous chapter. But other times that belief system is rooted in a faulty view of self.

We believe we are supposed to push through, and that not pushing through is a sign of weakness.

We believe we are the ones who have to do it all.

We believe we have to be all things to all people.

We believe our value and worth are tied to our productivity.

We believe we are supposed to suffer through life.

We believe we don't deserve to rest, take a break, or take care of ourselves.

> Spiritual commitment doesn't always translate into emotional health.

We carry a dangerously unhealthy view of our identity that then spills over into how we treat ourselves. Because oftentimes, the messages we've downloaded about ourselves and our identities are rooted in trauma rather than in God's truth.

This was exactly the case for Jeremy. He had allowed everything to pile on his shoulders. He was the yes-man for everyone around him. He believed the lie that he had to be the one to take care of the needs of everyone around him, at the neglect of his own needs. He believed the burden was his to carry, and that he didn't have the freedom, right, or permission to assess and assert his own needs. He may have never said those things out loud, but he was living in a way that affirmed this paradigm.

But how does a pastor of a thriving megachurch struggle with these types of beliefs? Here's why: Spiritual commitment doesn't always translate into emotional health. You can love Jesus, serve His people, and still have an unhealthy view of yourself. You can read your Bible and pray every day and still allow yourself to live out of a false identity. In order to bring our identity into alignment with God's truth, we often have to go back and confront some of the lies we've been believing. Lies that subtly make their way into our lives during the most vulnerable seasons, when we're most susceptible.

CONFRONTING THE LIES

I spent some time backtracking with Jeremy, helping him get to the roots of why he was so out of touch with his own capacity—of why he believed he didn't have permission to identify and express his needs. We did an activity together that I talk about in a few of my books, one I have almost all my clients do, called the timeline activity.[1] We talked through the different experiences in his life, from childhood to the present, that affirmed those beliefs to be "true." For Jeremy, much of these faulty beliefs began in childhood, long before he came to Jesus. Jeremy grew up in a chaotic home environment, with a stepdad who was angry, abusive, and authoritarian. His biological father had walked out on them at a young age, and all Jeremy knew of a father was this demanding man who ran the house like a military boot camp. If Jeremy ever disobeyed, the punishment was guaranteed to be severe, humiliating, and painful. He might get verbally shamed for a week straight, get locked in a room for 12 hours, have food withheld for longer than any young boy should have to endure, or even worse.

There was no room for error. He had lived his entire life ignoring his needs and desires because they really didn't matter. The only thing that mattered were the needs of his stepdad and doing things "his way," which was the only right way in that type of dysfunctional household. Experiences like this shape you. They shape your view of self, God, and others. They begin to inform what you believe, how you feel, and what you do as a result. And becoming a Christian doesn't automatically undo these difficult experiences, nor does it dismantle the beliefs that came as a result.

When Jeremy radically came to Jesus as a young man, a lot of that mental baggage came along with him. Even though he was instantly set free from his former life of addiction and sin—a miracle in and of itself—the mental battle still waged war on his life. He held on to some of the false beliefs from his childhood—namely that he had to obey and do things "the right way"—but this time, in his new belief system, he had to obey in order to please God. He had essentially replaced his stepdad with God. Mistakes were unacceptable. He had grown so accustomed to doing the best, being the best, and obeying in the best way he could that he pushed himself harder and faster and longer than anyone else he knew.

Not only that, but he had grown so accustomed to ignoring his own needs and focusing on the needs of his stepdad that he continued to live that way in his ministry as well. *Serving God is the only thing that matters*, he told himself. But what Jeremy didn't realize was how out of touch he was with his own human capacity and how he was hurting himself in the name of serving God. By ignoring his needs, he was ignoring his signals. All the alarms were going off, but he was too focused on the goal to even recognize what was happening—until it was too late, and he completely broke down.

"Do you realize that, in a way, you're continuing the cycle of abuse?" I gently confronted him one day in our sessions. "Except instead of being abused by your stepdad, you're the one abusing yourself."

He stared at me for a few moments, without even blinking. I couldn't read his blank face, and I wasn't sure how he was processing what I'd just said. Until a flood of tears came to his eyes and poured down his face for the very first time in our sessions. That revelation had hit him hard. He was so used to living a life under extreme pressure, with a high tolerance for suffering, that he was repeating the pattern without even realizing. This time, *he* was the one abusing himself. He was the one setting unrealistic standards. He was the one ignoring his needs and trying to exceed his capacity. In his efforts to push himself and even ignore himself, he was self-destructing.

Now he was starting to understand why even his "good life" felt so bad.

GETTING TO THE WHY

Each of us who struggles to care for ourselves well has an underlying motivation for *why* we don't. For Jeremy, his underlying beliefs that his feelings didn't matter pushed him to the point of suffering and pain—feelings he was very familiar with. For you, it might be the motivation to please the people around you, the fear of abandonment or rejection, an attempt at avoiding conflict and pursuing peace, or the fear of losing relationships. It could be that you believe you must be the one to fix things for everyone around you, because if *you* don't do it, no one else will. Maybe you grew up taking care of everyone else and never truly learned how to care for yourself. Maybe deep down you believe it's selfish to focus on your needs and desires because that's what you were told by someone significant in your life.

The question I want to ask you is *why*.

Why do you struggle to care for yourself?

What false beliefs, hurts, or lies might be leading you to live an empty life?

We can't go on to unpack *how* to care for ourselves until we answer the question of *why* we neglect to do so in the first place. Because it's not just about what we do; it's about why we do it. Right there, my friends, is the beginning of real change.

I could have easily given Jeremy a checklist of things to do to alleviate the burnout he was feeling. I could have told him to take some more time for himself, to spend extra time at the gym, or to take a nice long vacation. And let me assure you, there's a place for all those things. But if Jeremy didn't get to the root of his actions and begin confronting the lies that were causing him to live in such an unhealthy way, a few short-term solutions weren't going to take him very far. Without confronting the why, it would only be a matter of time until he defaulted back to self-destructive behaviors.

And the same goes for you. You have to get to the root of your *why*. Why has it been so difficult for you to set boundaries? To prioritize rest? To say no? To balance your schedule? To invest in filling up? To check in with how you're feeling and what you need? To tune in to your needs? What are some of the underlying motivations and beliefs that keep you stuck in a self-destructive and self-sabotaging pattern, and what lies do you need to confront to begin the process of healing? You might be thinking through this as you're reading these pages and finding yourself able to identify some of what has been holding you back, to identify some of the lies that need to be confronted. But maybe you're not totally sure. Maybe you know there's a problem, but you're having a harder time getting to the root of why. Or maybe, like Jeremy, you're too tired, depleted, and burned-out to even start to process the why. If either of these is the case, remember: You don't have to do this alone. Just like Jeremy sought the help of a counselor, so can you. I have an amazing team of Christian counselors who would be privileged and honored to help you on this journey, to walk with you until you are out the other side.[2]

GOD WANTS YOU TO BE FILLED

No matter what anyone or anything from your past may have told you, I hope you'll remember that God's will is for you to be filled. All over Scripture we see evidence of this truth. Ephesians 3:17-19 reminds

> God's will is for you to be filled.

us of this desire when it says, "I pray that you, being rooted and established in love, may have power, together with all the Lord's holy people, to grasp how wide and long and high and deep is the love of Christ, and to know this love that surpasses knowledge—that you may be filled to the measure of all the fullness of God." That you may be filled to the measure of all the fullness of God! Filled to the brim. Filled to overflowing. This is not something that happens automatically. This is something we must be intentional about in our lives.

I don't know where you are in your life today: whether you're feeling close to empty, living on fumes, about to break down, or just wanting to make sure you remain full. But no matter where you are and what you're going through in this season of life, I want to help you get to the root of the *why* so we can dive into the *what* to do about it—the practical steps of intentionally filling up. Because full people can fill people. Empty people can't. So let's get you filled to overflowing.

Verses for Reflection

I pray that you, being rooted and established in love, may have power, together with all the Lord's holy people, to grasp how wide and long and high and deep is the love of Christ, and to know this love that surpasses knowledge—that you may be filled to the measure of all the fullness of God (Ephesians 3:17-19).

Today's Rhythm: CONFRONT YOUR VIEW OF SELF

1. What is your *why*? What subtle or not-so-subtle lies have you believed about yourself that have prevented you from setting boundaries, saying no, setting limits, acknowledging your capacity, and caring for yourself? List them below.

2. Growing up, what were some of the messages you received—or didn't receive—about caring for yourself?

3. Do you believe it's God's will for you to be filled? Read Ephesians 5:8, Acts 2:4, and Ephesians 3:9, then write down reasons why you believe God wants you to live filled rather than empty.

4. "Spiritual commitment doesn't always translate into emotional health." After rereading this line from the chapter, write down the ways you have invested or will invest in your emotional health.

Chapter 5

EMPTY THINGS CAN'T FILL EMPTY PEOPLE

What's Not Working?

THE WORST KIND OF MEAL IS AN UNSATISFYING MEAL.
Before a trip, I like to do what I call the "pull everything out of the fridge and freezer and try to come up with a meal" activity. It not only fuels my creative streak to see what kind of dish I can come up with, but it also helps us to clean out the fridge before we leave town! We were getting ready to leave for a long stretch of vacation recently, so I started channeling my inner Food Network self by pretending I was on an episode of the TV show *Chopped*. I was throwing things together into what seemed like a cohesive meal, but halfway into the process, I had a feeling that maybe this wasn't such a good idea. Because there was no real plan or recipe and I was just going with what was available, the flavors and textures started competing with one another rather than complementing one another.

Now typically, I'm a pretty good cook (if I do say so myself), but the more I tried to add things to salvage this dish, the worse the dish got.

When it was time to finally sit down for dinner—let's just say everyone struggled, from the oldest to the youngest. It's amazing how you can be so hungry, yet the food you're putting in your mouth doesn't seem to do the trick of filling you up. Sure, it might take up space in your stomach, but it doesn't satisfy. "I've never felt so full yet so empty at the same time," my husband said after dinner, a dissatisfied grin on his face. And I had to laugh with him because there was no truer statement. It was seriously the most unsatisfying meal.

THINGS THAT DON'T SATISFY

We often do something similar in trying to fill up emotionally. When we start feeling even the slightest hint of emptiness, drain, and exhaustion, we can be tempted to run to a quick fix—something to give us a boost, distract us, or fill us up as fast as possible. We go to things hoping they will fill us up, but in the end, they don't. See if you can relate to any of these quick fixes:

- Running to the fridge for calories you don't need.

- Drinking even more caffeine to energize your unrested body.

- Opening a shopping app on your phone and spending money that's not in the budget.

- Binge-watching TV shows or gaming until late into the night when you should be sleeping.

- Mindlessly scrolling on your phone instead of being present with those around you.

- Going down a rabbit trail of random YouTube videos instead of staying on task.

- Running to unhealthy or toxic relationships, or even to sexual sin.

- Resorting to pornography, drugs, alcohol, or other substances to fill needs they were never meant to fill.

* Spending more time on ministry, work, or productivity to distract yourself, though it ends up draining you even more.

These choices leave us feeling more depleted in the end and perpetuate the cycle of feeling empty. Because empty things can't fill up empty people.

In Micah 6, we see God interacting with His people, the Israelites, who had strayed from the life-giving truths He'd given them. And He responds to them by saying, "You will eat but not be satisfied, for there will be hunger within you" (Micah 6:14 HCSB). When we try to fill up with our own methods, we're left empty and unsatisfied. We're left with a hunger still stirring within us. And yet, we keep going back for more of those very unsatisfying things.

> Empty things can't fill up empty people.

AN UNSATISFIED NATION

We're a very unsatisfied nation because we spend a lot of time and money on things that can't actually fill us up. Take a look at these staggering statistics to see just what we turn to:

* Each year, the average American spends $1,097 on coffee.[1]
* In 2023, Netflix's revenue was $33.7 billion dollars.[2]
* Every single *second*, $3,075.94 is spent on pornography. The porn industry makes $97 billion each year, which is more than "the combined revenues of ABC, NBC, and CBS and more than the combined revenues of NFL, NBA, and MLB."[3]
* The shopping platform Amazon gets over 2.72 billion unique visitors every month, with the typical American adult spending $50–100 per month.[4]
* The average working-age individual spends 2.5 hours on social media per day,[5] a number that seems to be increasing with each year.

- More people access pornography online each month than they visit Netflix, Amazon, and X (formerly Twitter) put together.[6]

- The average American spends more than $1,200 on fast food every year, which comes out to 10 percent of the average household daily income.[7]

- Millennials are spending an average of $300 per month on alcohol.[8]

- The average daily screen time in the USA is seven hours and five minutes.[9]

And we keep going back for more. We keep fueling the cycle of emptiness by running to empty things instead of seeking out what will truly satisfy our souls. In Isaiah 55:2, we're challenged with an important question: "Why spend money on what is not bread, and your labor on what does not satisfy? Listen, listen to me, and eat what is good, and you will delight in the richest of fare." Why are we spending our money, our energy, and our time on things that cannot fill us up? Substances, screens, sex, and spending don't have that kind of power! When will we realize that we are draining our souls rather than filling them up?

WHAT DO YOU RUN TO?

Let me ask you a question, and let's go ahead and make it personal: When you're drained and empty and depleted, what do *you* run to? What is your default method of filling up? I'll give you a hint: Most often our method is the thing we do as quickly as possible with whatever is available around us. It usually doesn't come with much prep or planning, and it often comes without much intention or deliberation. We typically choose something we can pick up quickly, turn to readily, engage in mindlessly, and do without really thinking about where it will lead us.

> Soul care is a rhythm we choose to engage—a path we choose to embark on.

But let me assure you, that is the exact opposite of soul care. Because soul care is intentional and thought-out. Soul care is a rhythm we choose to engage—a path we choose to embark on. It's a mapped-out plan, tried and tested by those who have gone before us. It's a journey that leads us to becoming healthier emotionally, mentally, physically, and spiritually— one intentional step at a time.

SOUL CARE

Today we've stopped to take inventory of what isn't working in our lives, of the things that aren't really filling us up. I'm not saying there's no place in our lives for coffee, Netflix, shopping, and fast food, but when we go to those things for our primary means of filling, we'll never be satisfied. So, over the next few sections of this book, we're going to do a deep dive into what *does* satisfy—things that can truly fill up our souls. We're on a journey of discovering six rhythms that, I believe, Jesus modeled for us during His time on this earth. Each of these rhythms is an intentional way of truly caring for our souls. Some of these rhythms are simple, and some are a little more complex, but each one is clearly evidenced in the life of Jesus—a man who deeply understood the nature of His humanity and invested in caring for His soul. And you know what? He cares for your soul as well because He loves you. You were created to live filled, so you can fully live.

Verse for Reflection

Why spend money on what is not bread, and your labor on what does not satisfy? Listen, listen to me, and eat what is good, and you will delight in the richest of fare (Isaiah 55:2).

Today's Rhythm: WHAT'S NOT WORKING?

1. Currently, what is your default way of filling up that doesn't actually fill you?

2. How much time do you spend each day on your screen (TV, phone, or other device)? (If you need a reference point, check your phone data or iPhone settings for screen time notifications.)

3. Are you currently using something to "fill up" that's unhealthy, damaging, or destructive? (For example: pornography, gambling, illegal drugs, alcohol abuse, unhealthy sexual behaviors, etc.)

4. Is there anything in your life that's not unhealthy in moderation, but can lead to wasted time, money, or energy? (For example: screen time, food, shopping, caffeine, social media, gaming, sugar consumption, etc.) Choose one default area you want to adjust. Write out the limits or boundaries you need to set around this specific habit in your life.

NOURISH

Caring for Your Soul Through Nutrition,
Hydration, and Movement

Chapter 6

COME AND EAT

Fuel Your Body Well

I READ AN ARTICLE ABOUT AN 87-YEAR-OLD WOMAN who fed her home intruder. A teenage boy had broken into her home around two a.m. He held her at knifepoint, but eventually, she fought him off. After the conflict, the boy told her he was "awfully hungry," so she took him to the kitchen and got him some peanut butter, a box of honey crackers, two protein shakes, and two tangerines. Then she sent him on his way like the sweet old lady she was. After that, she called the police.[1]

Aside from the absolute craziness of this story, my counselor brain can't help but wonder—would that teenage boy have done what he did if he wasn't so hungry? Addiction recovery groups all over the nation have an acronym they call HALT. It's a reminder that you're most susceptible to making poor decisions when you're *hungry, angry, lonely,* or *tired.* HALT is an encouragement not to neglect your personal needs, and it emphasizes the need to fuel your body well.

We get a personal taste of this when we get "hangry." Our blood sugar drops, which impacts our serotonin levels, and we often find our mood shifting toward the negative: cranky, irritable, angry, etc. Research has shown notable shifts in mood when people neglect to fuel themselves, because the brain "doesn't function properly in low glucose states."[2] Those heightened negative emotions act like our body's alarm, reminding us to bring our body back to baseline because we're long overdue! I don't know about you, but it makes me wonder how many things we subtly do out of "hanger" that may have otherwise been avoided had we adequately maintained and nourished our bodies.

NOURISH YOUR BODY

Let me tell you a little secret.

It's a small piece of advice that just might rock your world. It's a nugget of truth that isn't usually preached from the pulpit nor outlined in the best theology books—yet it's crystal clear within the truths of Scripture. Here it is:

Some of the most soul-filling practices you can do for yourself aren't spiritual practices at all. Because God created us as intricate, holistic human beings made in His image, each part of us impacts the whole.

When the teachers of the law asked Jesus to tell them the greatest commandment, without hesitation, Jesus said:

> The most important one…is this: "Hear, O Israel: The Lord our God, the Lord is one. Love the Lord your God with all your heart and with all your soul and with all your mind and with all your strength" (Mark 12:29-31).

Heart. Soul. Mind. Strength.

Emotional health. Spiritual health. Mental health. Physical health.

Feelings, emotions, mind, and body.

It's all connected!

Jesus was clear to identify the four quadrants by which we can love God. I write extensively about these quadrants of health in my book *Are You Really OK?* because I deeply believe that each of these areas greatly impacts the whole. Jesus wants us to love God with *every part of our being*, yet we often fixate on the spiritual aspects while neglecting all the other components to caring for ourselves.

But part of loving God well means loving God with all our strength, which comes down to the practice of caring for our bodies. It may sound so "unspiritual," but it's crucial to functioning effectively and getting the most out of life. When your body is not at its best, it often limits your ability to fully walk in your God-given calling. It's hard to go to "Jerusalem, and in all Judea and Samaria, and to the ends of the earth" when we are weak, tired, and sick because of the way we've neglected our bodies (Acts 1:8).

> Some of the most soul-filling practices you can do for yourself aren't spiritual practices at all.

One of the most basic (yet often neglected) practices of soul care that Jesus modeled for us involves nourishing our bodies—fueling them with the proper nutrition and hydration to keep them going and to keep them strong. When was the last time you heard a sermon about taking care of your body?

While it may be underdiscussed in church, it's highlighted in Scripture by the way Jesus lived His life. Jesus did not neglect His body. He took the time for important daily disciplines such as eating and drinking! We often take this for granted, but our bodies were made to be fueled in order to function at their best. There are numerous passages in Scripture about Jesus taking time to eat (Luke 11:37), urging His disciples to eat (John 21:12), sitting around a table and sharing a meal (Luke 7:36), or having a meal prepared for Him (John 12:2). Luke 7:34 even says that the "Son of Man came eating and drinking," which is not what people expected of the Messiah! His human nature came with important human needs that required His attention.

I especially love that Jesus stopped to make sure His disciples were eating. "Come and have breakfast," He told them (John 21:12). I love this side of Jesus so much because it absolutely resonates with my Middle Eastern background. Coming from an Egyptian family, I learned one of my parents' love languages is feeding people. Growing up, I could assure you that if you came to visit our house, it was a guarantee that you would eat. There was no way around it and no way out of it. Making sure people were nourished and well-fed was (and still is) a really important part of Middle Eastern culture. And there wasn't just enough food to feed the family; there was always more than enough in case we had unexpected visitors—or in case the mail service worker or UPS delivery person happened to come by right around mealtime. (I kid you not, they offered food to everyone.) We could have ten unexpected guests come by, and there would still be enough. "Come and eat!" I can't tell you how many times I heard that phrase, spoken in my mom's Middle Eastern accent. It makes me smile as I imagine Jesus, bright and early that morning, urging His disciples: "Come and eat!"

In contrast, I look at some of the cultural norms I'm surrounded by today. I live in Lancaster, Pennsylvania. Lancaster is known as the "home of the Amish" and is heavily populated by the Amish and Mennonite communities. One thing that is strong in this cultural template is a hard work ethic, which spills over into the lives of the entire community. People around here know how to get things done—to work hard and work long. It's not uncommon for people to work long hours and then find even more projects to work on during their time off. A phrase I hear often around here is, "I forgot to eat today!" People are literally working so hard, immersed in what they're doing, that they forget to stop and eat! I don't know if it's a Lancaster thing or what, but how can you forget to eat? Although my Middle Eastern brain can't compute that, I wouldn't be surprised if some of you have been guilty of neglecting to nourish your bodies. I wouldn't be surprised if you've fallen into a cycle of putting your physical needs on the back burner while you focus on more "important" goals.

Sometimes, in an attempt to do more, we actually set ourselves up to do less. We go-go-go to the point of neglecting our undernourished bodies. And then we feel awful when our blood sugar drops, which then impacts our serotonin and dopamine levels. We get moody as a result, and hangry, and irritable, and then we think we're under some sort of spiritual attack! When really, we've simply neglected to nourish ourselves.

It's amazing how much we can overspiritualize our negative experiences, when sometimes those experiences and feelings are simply the body signaling to us a very basic human need: We need to stop and care for ourselves, to nourish our bodies with healthy food, to stay hydrated, and to fuel ourselves with the nutrition that our bodies need to function most effectively.

WHAT WOULD JESUS EAT?

While doing some research on the concept of nourishment, I decided to Google the phrase "what would Jesus eat?" just to see what might come up in a search. I found a fascinating book that I've been digging into recently, titled *What Would Jesus Eat?* The author, a board-certified family medicine physician, examines the eating habits of Jesus, applying some of those healthy eating principles to how we should feed and fuel our bodies today. It's a fascinating look at the benefits of unprocessed whole foods, which are rich in vitamins and nutrients. After he does a deep dive into the eating habits of Jesus and unpacks the Levitical dietary laws, the author concludes that our bodies function best with three simple things: whole foods, fresh foods, and foods without pesticides, fungicides, and additives.[3] Contrast that to the top three foods consumed in America—white bread, coffee, and hot dogs—and you'll notice we have quite a long way to go when it comes to fueling our bodies well.

Don't worry. I'm not about to get all extreme on you with a list of detailed rules and regulations about what you should and should not eat. Because this isn't about adding more rules to our lives; it's simply about learning to nourish ourselves in the best way possible. The Bible makes it clear that even though we have freedom, we also have the responsibility to decide that some things are simply not beneficial to

> The Bible makes it clear that even though we have freedom, we also have the responsibility to decide that some things are simply not beneficial to our lives.

our lives. First Corinthians 10:23 reminds us, "You say, 'I am allowed to do anything'—but not everything is good for you. You say, 'I am allowed to do anything'—but not everything is beneficial" (NLT). Especially when it comes to the way we fuel our bodies, we need to remind ourselves that though something may be allowed, we should also ask ourselves: Is it beneficial?

It's no small problem to note that obesity has reached epidemic proportions in the United States, with over 60 percent of people falling into that category.[4] We are at our heaviest as a nation, yet all the while, we're also lacking in essential vitamins and nutrients. We're overweight yet undernourished. I think we can all agree that we are fueling ourselves in a way that's causing a national health crisis and leading us to chronic illness and disease.

The reason I hesitate to include a list of what to eat and what *not* to eat is because I don't believe in black-and-white answers to this concept of fueling our bodies well. I know many well-respected people in the nutrition and health industry who are fueling their bodies with a variety of different diets—from low-carb to gluten-free, from sugar-free to keto, from whole foods to vegetarianism and veganism, and everything in between. There are organic, free-range, grass-fed, grass-finished, whole-grained, non-GMO, and so many other options that it can easily become overwhelming—and then we end up doing nothing. Which is why I don't want to overcomplicate this. The key here isn't to jump on the latest trend; it's to be intentional in the daily choices we make with regard to what we put into our bodies.

While there are so many food guidelines out there, and while it's important to do some research for yourself to find what fuels your body in a way that works for you,[5] here are a few broad principles that I've found to be important and helpful in my personal life and journey of nourishing my body:

- **Nutrients:** Rather than focusing on types of food or food group categories, and rather than seeing food in terms of *good* or *bad*, look at the nutritional value of the foods you eat instead. The higher the nutritional value, the better it is for your body. Fuel your body with the foods that have sufficient amounts of the nutrients your body needs to function at its best. Our mental health is intertwined with our physical health, so fueling your body well will also fuel your mind well.

* **Balance:** Focus on balance when it comes to how you fuel your body, with a variety of fruits and vegetables, whole grains and nutritional carbohydrates, healthy fats and proteins, with treats in moderation. Not only is balance important for getting the nutritional value that you need, but it also helps to maintain a healthy approach long-term. I love the concept they teach kids of trying to "eat the rainbow" every day. When it comes to a balanced diet, look for God-created whole foods of every color. (Natural colors, of course! Like I had to remind my seven-year-old, that bright red 7-Eleven Slurpee and that pack of Skittles don't count!) The blander your plate looks in color, the less balanced it likely is.

* **Energy:** Remember that the main reason you fuel your body is so you can have the energy and strength to function at your best. Be in tune with your body and *when* it needs to be fueled! Be consistent with your meals and don't forget to feed yourself because you "got too busy." Not only that, but be aware of the amount of energy you are expending and make sure it aligns with the amount of energy you're taking in. Overdoing it in either direction (giving your body less than it needs or more than it needs) will keep you from feeling and functioning at your best. Find out your daily caloric needs based on your energy expenditure, and consistently remain within those limits.

* **Moderation:** As we mentioned earlier, with freedom comes responsibility. I generally disagree with the idea of putting any

food in the "bad" category—except maybe for pork rinds. I'll never understand the allure of deep-fried pigskin! But all jokes aside, I try to avoid using language that vilifies food altogether because I deeply believe in the concept of moderation. Proverbs reminds us that even too much of a good thing can end up being a bad thing. I like how The Message puts it: "When you're given a box of candy, don't gulp it all down; eat too much chocolate and you'll make yourself sick" (Proverbs 25:16). No matter what you're eating, one thing is clear: Healthy moderation is key. If you're going to have a treat food versus a nourishing food, see it as just that and set limits around your consumption. Because even though it's permissible, it may not be beneficial.

The takeaway is simple: Don't neglect to nourish your body. Ultimately, we have to steward our bodies well as a means of honoring God. We want to fuel our bodies out of a place of honor, not out of a place of shame.

HONORING YOUR TEMPLE

I think it's safe to say that too many of us have been taught to shame our bodies rather than to honor them. We look down on our bodies instead of feeling proud of them. But the cycle of shame always leads us away from the path of health. When we are cynical, negative, critical, and constantly degrading to ourselves, our emotions respond accordingly. And when you're filled with sadness, frustration, discouragement, and hopelessness, you're more likely to make choices that lead you away from health rather than toward it.

> We want to fuel our bodies out of a place of honor, not out of a place of shame.

The most motivating thing you can do for yourself is to honor your body with gratitude. Gratitude that God made you strong. Gratitude that your body is made in the most wonderful way (Psalm 139:14). Gratitude for the miracles of living and breathing and moving (Acts 17:28). And above all, gratitude to a God who knows every detail on your body, every single hair on your head, and exactly how you were formed (Luke 12:7). When you honor your body, you're honoring the temple God resides in. So listen and respond as Jesus says, "Come and eat," and fuel your body well.

Verse for Reflection

Whether you eat or drink or whatever you do,
do it all for the glory of God (1 Corinthians 10:31).

Today's Rhythm: FUEL YOUR BODY WELL

1. We learned that the top three most consumed foods in America are white bread, coffee, and hot dogs. With that in mind, if you had to guess, what are your top three most consumed foods?

2. On a scale of zero to ten, how much intention do you put into the idea of nourishing your body with nutritious foods? (Zero being: "I don't really think about nutrition and eat whatever I feel like eating." Ten being: "I assess every food that enters my body.")

3. Out of the four principles of healthy eating mentioned in this chapter—nutrients, balance, energy, and moderation—which one comes the hardest for you?

4. What are some steps you can take to honor God with how you fuel yourself this coming week? How can you begin to apply some of these goals and principles to your daily life?

Chapter 7

IT MIGHT NOT BE A DEMON

Don't Forget to Hydrate

I WAS OUT OF TOWN RECENTLY ON A MINISTRY TRIP TO Nashville. Since I tend to travel a lot, my husband tries to join me as often as his schedule will allow, but this time I had to travel alone for a quick two-day trip to the Music City. It was a full 48 hours, including an eight-hour recording day for a national TV program followed by a podcast interview the next day. The first day on set for the TV show was packed with filming, conversations, and photo shoots, so I didn't have much time to stop and hydrate. Frankly, I didn't think much of it.

I got a really good night's sleep, so I was surprised when the next morning, as soon as I opened my eyes, I felt my heart pounding out of my chest. It was thumping so loud and so fast I could almost hear it in my ears. It sounded like the beating of a loud drum. Trying to remain calm, I slowly made my way to the bathroom to grab my watch so I could use the built-in heart rate monitor. When I put on my watch and looked at my heart rate, it had reached 187 beats per minute! At this point, I started to panic and quickly called my friend. She had also been on the TV program with me the day before, and thanks be to God, she was staying in the same hotel in the room right next door. She rushed over to help me and sat me back down on the bed. She got me some water, and I proceeded to call my husband, who asked me some questions and talked me through next steps. (Sidenote: It's so convenient to be married to a doctor!)

"Do you feel like you're going to pass out?" he asked.

"No, I'm okay."

"Are you having any chest pain?" he continued.

"No, no pain."

"Any other symptoms?"

"No, just this crazy heart rate," I responded.

"Okay…in that case, keep watching your heart rate, avoid caffeine today, and drink plenty of water! Then call me if it gets worse."

I hung up the phone. Although this didn't feel like anxiety, I tried to calm my mind and do some of the breathing exercises I typically practice whenever I'm feeling anxious. My sweet friend (thank God for sisters in Christ!) stayed with me for the next hour, playing worship songs on her phone while I lay down in bed and waited for my heart rate to return to normal. The more I thought about it, I realized I hadn't had enough water the day before—if any. I recalled drinking a couple sips of water here and there throughout the day. But could this really be from dehydration? It felt like a stretch. Still, I committed to hydrating for the rest of that day. I felt better as the day went on, got through my interview, and then flew home later that night feeling totally normal. But the memory of my pounding heart rate still lingered in my mind.

When I got home, we set up a series of appointments with the cardiologists in town. They had me do all kinds of tests to check my heart. I had to wear a heart monitor for two weeks, and even had an electrical study done on my heart. Finally, all the results came in, and the conclusion was this: I have a very healthy heart! Thank God for that. But it still didn't explain what happened in Nashville. "Your heart rate seems to spike periodically," said the cardiologist at my follow-up appointment. "Most likely it was a combination of hormonal changes and dehydration."

IT MIGHT NOT BE A DEMON

I truly believe the enemy can use our weak spots at just the right times to hold us back from all God has called us to do. I certainly believe there was a spiritual component to my not feeling well during my ministry trip, and I have seen that pattern consistently over the years. Whenever I'm planning or preparing for a big ministry event, something inevitably comes up to distract or derail me. The strangest and most random things have happened before or during my time away. One time, the morning before a big speaking engagement, a sudden respiratory virus landed us in the emergency room at two a.m. because my youngest son was having a hard time breathing. (Praise the Lord, he was okay! And praise the Lord that He ministered through me in a powerful way even through my sleep deprivation the night before!) Another time, as we were loading up in our car to drive to the airport, we opened the door to get in and noticed the most bizarre fly infestation inside—almost like the plagues on Egypt during Moses's day. (Though we're still not sure how that one happened, I don't think being Egyptian had anything to do with it!)

Yet another time while we were away, the glass shower in our bathroom blew up, shattering into a million pieces in the middle of the night. (Thank God the kids weren't in there at the time!) But the worst was when I was en route to speak at a wide-reaching church in Montana, and a cancelled flight landed me in a reputable Chicago hotel that ended up having bedbugs! Worse yet, I found out I have a *massive* allergic reaction to bedbug bites. It was awful. I had itchy, hot, painful baseball-sized welts all over my body for the next week and was traumatized by hotel beds for the next three years. I'm telling you, the enemy has often used the most random things to distract and derail me. But you'd better believe that I won't let him!

But here's what I also believe: Sometimes we overspiritualize our situation instead of seeing our role and responsibility in it. Some of the unexpected things I just mentioned were out of my own hands, but the morning in Nashville was *partially* the result of my own self-neglect. I should have been hydrating! I should have cared enough about my body to take care of it. I should have understood that these small practices make a big difference in how my body responds and functions. My friend Levi Lusko said it best when, in the foreword to one of my books, he wrote about our tendency to focus on the spiritual while neglecting all the other aspects of our health: "In the church we can be guilty of looking for spiritual solutions to physical or emotional problems. You might not have a demon—you might just be dehydrated."[1]

While I firmly believe the enemy is always ready to steal, kill, and destroy, I also believe we often *expose* ourselves by neglecting to protect what God has given us! We make ourselves even more vulnerable and susceptible to attack when we're not protecting ourselves. When Peter warns us that the enemy is prowling around like a lion waiting to devour someone, he also reminds us that the antidote of that attack is to "be alert and of sober mind" (1 Peter 5:8). This tells me that we are not powerless to the antics of the enemy. We can protect our spirits by putting on the full armor of God, and we can also protect our bodies by being alert and taking care of ourselves in the best ways we can. Because at the end of the day, it might not be a demon—you might just need to drink more water! My situation was evidence of that.

BIBLICAL HYDRATION

The importance of water is referenced many, many times throughout Scripture. In fact, it's mentioned 722 times in the Bible, more often than faith, hope, prayer, and worship.[2] Water is used as an analogy to point to the Spirit of God. Isaiah 44:3 says,

> I will pour water on the thirsty land, and streams on the dry ground; I will pour out my Spirit on your offspring, and my blessing on your descendants.

Again, in John 7:37-38, we read the words of Jesus:

> Let anyone who is thirsty come to me and drink. Whoever believes in me, as Scripture has said, rivers of living water will flow from within them.

Water is also used to represent eternal life, as we see in Isaiah 12:3: "With joy you will draw water from the wells of salvation." It's used to depict the idea of cleansing, as in Hebrews 10:22: "having our hearts sprinkled to cleanse us from a guilty conscience and having our bodies washed with pure water." It's used to represent God's Word, as in Ephesians 5:26: "having cleansed her by the washing of water with the word" (ESV).

But not only is there spiritual significance to the idea of water in Scripture. There's also practical and physical significance. Water cleanses and purifies, *and* it nourishes our bodies. The Bible often references God taking care of His people by providing both food and water. For example: "They will neither hunger nor thirst, nor will the desert heat or the sun beat down on them. He who has compassion on them will guide them and lead them beside springs of water" (Isaiah 49:10).

When God called Elijah to prophesy to King Ahab, He told him to hide in the Kerith Ravine and drink from the brook (1 Kings 17:3-4). He made sure not only to provide food for Elijah through the ravens, but also to provide exact instructions for where he would get water to drink! When leaving Egypt for the promised land, the Israelites found the water along their journey to be bitter and undrinkable. So God gave Moses instructions to procure fresh water that was good to drink (Exodus 15:22-25). Later, God provided fresh water for them to flow from a rock by Mount Horeb (Exodus 17:1-7).

We see God's provision through water in Scripture, but we also see Jesus Himself taking the time to stop for a drink. The phrase "give me a drink" is found nine times throughout the Bible, said by many people from David to Jesus to the prophets. In John 4 we see Jesus on a long journey from Judea to Galilea, when He stopped for a rest in Samaria:

> [Jesus] left Judea and went back once more to Galilee. Now he had to go through Samaria. So he came to a town in Samaria called Sychar…Jacob's well was there, and Jesus, tired as he was from the journey, sat down by the well. It was about noon. When a Samaritan woman came to draw water, Jesus said to

her, "Will you give me a drink?" (His disciples had gone into the town to buy food) (John 4:3-8).

Although I believe there was a much deeper purpose to His interaction with the Samaritan woman—He wanted to introduce her to the true Living Water that was sitting right beside her—I can't help but consider the humbling reality that if Jesus, who was both fully God and fully man, had human needs to eat and drink, how much more do I? He was tired, so He stopped to rest and specifically asked for a drink. He was thirsty and wanted to refresh His body, all while taking the time to refresh her soul. What a beautiful exchange.

Later, after a life well lived, as He endured the pain and suffering of the cross, bearing the consequence for our sins, He recognized that His body was in need of water when He said, "I am thirsty" (John 19:28). Though we know that through these words—one of seven significant final statements Jesus made before His death—Jesus was fulfilling the prophecy of Psalm 22:15, I believe we often fail to simply see Jesus's humanity in these simple words. He was thirsty, and His body was crying out for refreshment. Jesus was human. He got thirsty. And He knew His body needed water to drink.

STAY HYDRATED

You'd be surprised how many hilarious memes there are out there about staying hydrated. Here are some of the ones that got me laughing.

- Sometimes I drink water just to surprise my liver.
- Don't forget to drink water and get some sun. You're basically a houseplant with more complicated emotions.
- Why be mad when you can be hydrated?
- I look this good because I drink water.
- If you like water, then you already like most of me!
- If you drink a gallon of water a day, you won't have time for

other people's drama because you will be too busy peeing. Stay hydrated, my friends.

* The human body is 75 percent water. We're basically just cucumbers with anxiety!

That one about cucumbers actually got a laugh-out-loud chuckle out of me. Needless to say, water is vital to our existence. W.H. Auden once wrote: "Thousands have lived without love, not one without water."[3] According to an article from the Harvard University blog, between 60 and 75 percent of our weight is made up of water; and "a loss of just 4% of total body water leads to dehydration, and a loss of 15% can be fatal. Likewise, a person could survive a month without food but wouldn't survive 3 days without water."[4] We can all recognize our need for water, but why is it so necessary?

Not only does water consumption prevent dehydration, but it also helps you think clearly, stabilizes your mood, maintains your body's proper temperature, protects your spinal cord and other sensitive areas, lubricates your joints, prevents kidney stones and constipation, and gets rid of waste through urination and perspiration.[5] Water is especially vital for our brains. According to the American College of Nutrition, being dehydrated by just 2 percent impairs your ability to focus and pay attention, decreases your memory and recall, impacts your assessment and judgment, and effects your psychomotor abilities (your movements).[6] Your brain is made up of 85 percent water, so if a 2 percent rate of dehydration can impact you to that degree, imagine how much more our brains are impaired from optimal functioning when we're seriously dehydrated. The brain is the center of functioning. It controls our mood, our emotions, our thinking and cognition, our energy and focus, and so many other things. When our brain is not functioning properly due to dehydration, it impacts every part of us. One study showed that people who were hydrated had a 14 percent increase in reaction time compared to people who were not hydrated![7] Not only that, but when it comes to mood, dehydration impedes the production of serotonin in your body (the feel-good chemical), which can lead to sadness, depression, and increased anxiety.

Additionally, when your brain is not getting enough water, your energy levels drop.

The more we understand about the importance of hydration on every part of our being, the more it makes sense that Jesus stopped to take a drink. He knew water was essential to His body's optimal functioning. Yet so often, we underestimate our own need to stay hydrated and end up suffering for it.

When our brain is not functioning properly due to dehydration, it impacts every part of us.

Dehydration occurs when we're not getting the amount of water we need. The signs of dehydration are obvious, but we're not always looking for them. I mentioned earlier one of the signs of dehydration on my trip to Nashville came in the form of heart palpitations (a rapid heart rate). This is also known as a tachycardia episode, which is when your heart rate goes above 100 beats per minute. When you're dehydrated, your heart has to work harder to pump blood to the rest of your body, which causes an increased heart rate.[8] Some signs of dehydration include:

- Irritability or restlessness
- Rapid pulse
- Sunken eyes
- Feeling thirsty
- Pinched skin goes back slowly
- Dark yellow urine
- Weak pulse, lethargy, and difficulty breathing in cases of severe dehydration[9]

First, recognize the signs of dehydration. But even more importantly, prevent it by drinking plenty of water. Medical experts recommend drinking a minimum of a half-ounce of water for each pound you weigh. This means if you weigh 160 pounds, you should be drinking 80 ounces of water *minimum*. That's at least ten cups of water per day, or five 16-ounce bottles of water. The majority of people aren't getting anywhere near the amount of hydration they should be getting per day. Additionally, it's important to limit the amount of caffeine we're taking in per day, since caffeine is a diuretic—meaning it *removes* liquid from our body. Another tip for staying hydrated: Have a big container of water around at all times. Take small sips as a habit throughout the day rather than waiting until you feel thirsty.

As a mom of four, I've always noticed that when a sippy cup is available, a little one will constantly grab it to drink without thinking much of it. A child's natural instinct is to drink. We just have to make water available to them. I wonder if we need to do something similar as adults. Keep water within reach so it's easy and convenient to drink throughout the day! The best thing I did for myself after my palpitation episode was to buy a 40-ounce thermos that I am constantly sipping on throughout the day. I try to fill it up at least twice to make sure I'm getting 80 ounces of water each day. And I feel so much better when I do.

> It might not be a demon…you might just be dehydrated.

OBEY YOUR THIRST

It's too bad a water company didn't coin the phrase "obey your thirst" back in 1994 before Sprite laid claim to it. Because the truth is, we *should* obey our thirst. Our thirst is an indicator that our body is lacking in something it desperately needs. Instead of waiting to thirst, what if we were to honor our bodies by doing what Jesus did on earth and taking the time to stop and hydrate? Because it might not be a demon…you might just be dehydrated.

Verse for Reflection
Jesus said to her, "Will you give me a drink?" (John 4:7).

Today's Rhythm: DON'T FORGET TO HYDRATE

1. How many ounces of water do you currently drink per day?

2. Is hydration something you consider as an act of soul care? Why or why not? If not, has this chapter begun to shift your perspective on hydration?

3. Dehydration impacts our physical, emotional, and mental well-being. How have you noticed dehydration impacting you in a negative way?

4. According to the experts, you should be drinking half your weight in ounces of water per day. Calculate how many ounces you need based on your weight. Then think through some ways you can make drinking more water simple, easy, and attainable. (For example, drink one glass of water first thing in the morning, carry a thermos throughout the day, drink a glass of water before and during meals, etc.)

Chapter 8

WALKING WITH JESUS

Your Relationship with Movement

MY WATCH STARTED TO BUZZ A FEW MINUTES AGO,
alerting me that it was time to stand up. Apparently I've been sitting around
way too long today writing this book, so I took a quick break to stretch and
move around a little. So far today, I've only gotten 1,423 out of my suggested
10,000 daily steps. That's .61 miles that I've walked today. Since this is one
of my writing days, I'll spend a lot of time sitting rather than moving. I'll
have to get creative if I want to move my body the way it needs to be moved
today. But I'm realizing that moving my body is a gift. Moving my body,
a body that is currently healthy and strong, is something that I often take
for granted. Movement is, in fact, one of the ways I honor my body as well
as my mind, making sure both stay healthy and strong as long as possible.

In our society of shortcuts and conveniences, we often find the most
efficient way to get from A to Z without necessarily finding the *best* way. I
was at a sushi restaurant recently that had a conveyer belt of food next to
the table, so you didn't have to inconvenience yourself by standing up to
get what you wanted—the small plates of food would just pass you by, and

you could grab them on demand. Talk about an unnecessary—though I'll admit very fun—convenience. Everything is fast-paced and time-saving rather than deliberate and intentional. We don't even have to walk a mile down the road because, with the click of a button, we can catch an Uber. This is so drastically different from the culture Jesus lived in, where walking was pretty much the only option for anyone other than the rich and royal. So it makes sense that one of the healthy rhythms of Jesus during His time here on earth was movement! He moved...a lot.

When we hear the phrase "walking with Jesus," we automatically think about living for God. But as I've thought more about this concept, I've realized that the disciples were both literally and figuratively walking with Jesus during His time with them. So much of Scripture portrays Jesus and His disciples walking from one town to the next and back. They walked from Jerusalem and Nazareth (a distance of 85 miles) to get to His childhood home; they walked to Philippi, Capernaum, Cana of Galilee (to attend a wedding), the Sea of Galilee (where He walked on water), Jerusalem (for the Passover celebrations), the Jordan River (where He was baptized by John the Baptist), Bethany (the home of His friends Martha, Mary, and Lazarus), and Bethesda (where He healed the paralytic by the pool). And those are just some of the places He walked that are still in existence today if you were to visit Israel.[1]

Most biblical experts agree that Jesus likely walked 20 miles each day, which comes out to about 44,222 steps per day! That blows my 10,000 steps goal right out of the water. But here's why this matters: Movement is one of the ways we honor our bodies. It's one way we keep them healthy, strong, and resilient. And because most of us don't naturally walk long distances today, we have to intentionally integrate a rhythm of healthy movement in order to keep our bodies functioning at their best.

MOVEMENT AND MENTAL HEALTH

We can all agree that physical movement has a positive effect on the health of our bodies. In fact, movement is one of the most important things we can do for our physical health. We know exercise and movement strengthen our bones and muscles, help us manage our weight, and combat health conditions such as diabetes, stroke, blood pressure, arthritis, and many types of cancer.[2] But do you understand the significant power that movement also has on your mental health?

According to Harvard Health Publishing, regular movement and exercise decreases your body's fight-or-flight response, decreasing and alleviating the stored-up stress in your body.[3] Simply put, walking regulates your nervous system. Such a simple act can have a profound effect on your body's stress levels. All that stress and pressure has to go somewhere, and movement is one of the best ways to naturally release it from your system. Regular movement can also alleviate the symptoms of depression, and in some cases, can be as effective as medication and psychotherapy.[4] When we pair exercise and movement with other treatments, we see a very positive impact on our mental health. In fact, many studies have shown that walking, in and of itself, can significantly reduce symptoms of depression.[5] So those who walk more often struggle less with symptoms of depression than those who don't walk. Many of these studies found this to be true even up to three years after the study's completion.[6] Part of the reason walking is effective is because consistent movement for 30 minutes is another way to naturally increase the production of serotonin (that feel-good chemical we talked about earlier).[7] The health of our body has a direct impact on the health of our mind.

BODY CARE

When I look at the life of Jesus, I don't see someone who neglected the care of His body; I see someone who honored His body. As my friend, pastor and author Gary Thomas says,

> The health of our body has a direct impact on the health of our mind.

Body care is an aspect of Christian discipleship and worship.[8]

Second Corinthians 7:1 puts it like this in The Message translation:

> With promises like this to pull us on, dear friends, let's make a clean break with everything that defiles or distracts us, both

within and without. Let's make our entire lives fit and holy
temples for the worship of God.

Our entire lives should be fit and holy temples for the worship of God!
What if we started applying this verse to the way we care for our bodies?
Don't get me wrong. I recognize that for many of us, this isn't an easy
ask. We're tired after a long day of work. We're mentally and emotionally
strained. Our jobs are demanding, our kids are demanding, and our relationships are demanding. We don't know how or when we'll find the time
to care for our bodies, much less everything else that needs to be cared for
in our lives. But what if this physical discipline also has a spiritual benefit?
What if, in learning how to make those daily sacrifices—moving when we
feel tired, walking when we'd rather be sitting, exercising when we'd pre-
fer to be sedentary—we're actually disciplining our spirits as well? Gary
Thomas goes on to say,

> Body care requires immediate sacrifice for delayed rewards...but
> just think about how that shapes us into a certain kind of per-
> son that's willing to sacrifice today for spiritual benefits tomor-
> row. See, it not only affects [this], but it also affects the way we
> handle our finances, it affects the way we parent, the way we
> work in relationships, the way we work in ministry and evange-
> lism. Being willing to sacrifice today, to have an eternal perspec-
> tive. That we work today, even when we don't see the rewards,
> because we know that God's rewards are eternal. It changes
> who we are.[9]

IN HIM WE LIVE AND MOVE

Gary's words resonate with me because I love the idea of pairing physical disciplines with spiritual rewards. I find it much more motivating to
connect the care of my body with the care of my spirit. When I decided
to go on a 40-day sugar fast a few years ago, refraining from consuming
all refined sugars, I found it so much more inspiring to view it as a spiritual fast and run to God for my cravings rather than to sugar. In fact, with

this idea in mind, I was able to go well beyond the 40 days, which would have been much harder for me without the deeper spiritual meaning. Ultimately, I truly believe it's all connected—the mind, body, and spirit. When we care for one, we also impact the others.

When I think of caring for and nourishing my body through movement, I think of the verse that says, "For in him we live and move and have our being" (Acts 17:28). In Him we *move*. Every step I take, I can take for Him. Every movement my body makes, I can make it for Him. Every time I walk, or swim, or hike, or play pickleball, or jump on the trampoline with my kids, or go for a bike ride, or kayak down a canal, or lift weights in my basement...I'm doing it for Him. I'm moving as an act of worship to the God who made my body and knows just what it needs to thrive.

Consider how you can incorporate this perspective in your rhythm of movement each day. Since walking is something you can fit into any amount of time you have, maybe take a daily prayer walk for 5, 15, or 30 minutes. Walk around your neighborhood, praying for those God brings to your mind. Or maybe consider going for a jog, hike, run, or swim with some worship music in your ears, lifting your heart up as you lift up your body in movement. Go for a bike ride and tune in to a favorite sermon, or an audiobook or podcast to encourage your spirit. Pair your physical disciplines of movement with your spiritual growth, and watch how it increases your motivation.

One of the most basic yet practical ways we can care for our souls is by caring for the bodies God has given us. It starts with a heart of gratitude for our body and a desire to honor God by honoring His temple. We prepare ourselves for the calling God has given us by nourishing

> Every movement my body makes, I can make it for Him.

our bodies well in what we eat and drink and in how we move. This is the beginning of soul care. So let's start walking with Jesus. Literally.

Verse for Reflection

For in him we live and move and have our being (Acts 17:28).

Today's Rhythm: YOUR RELATIONSHIP WITH MOVEMENT

1. Reflect on today's verse. Have you ever considered the idea that body care is an act of worship to God? What are some ways you can incorporate basic movement into your daily routine?

2. If you don't know where to begin, consider this: How many steps do you take each day? Set a goal for yourself (with the help of your doctor or fitness trainer). If this is new for you, maybe consider starting with 4,000 steps each day, and working your way up to the recommended 10,000 steps per day.

3. Does the idea of connecting the act of physical movement with spiritual reward resonate with you? If so, what are some ways you can incorporate movement into how you worship and connect with God? (For example, a worship dance class, a daily prayer walk, praise and worship while running, etc.)

4. One of the most basic ways to care for your soul is to care for your body. With that in mind, how will you move your body *today*?

REST

✝

Caring for Your Soul Through Rhythms
of Rest and a Sustainable Pace of Life

Chapter 9

JESUS TOOK NAPS

Permission to Sleep

"THE WORD BECAME FLESH AND SLEPT AMONG US."[1]
One day that quote really caught my attention. Did you ever contemplate the fact that out of His 33 years on this earth, Jesus spent approximately 11 years of it sleeping? Something about the idea of Jesus sleeping for 11 years of His earthly days really puts things in perspective for me. Jesus took the time to rest—to close His eyes, lay down His head, still His thoughts, and sleep. Even though Jesus was fully God, He was also fully man. He understood the limitations of His human body and took the time to care for it by resting and recharging. Yet somehow, we—who are only fully human—tend to downplay our need to rest and recharge.

We human beings should spend approximately one-third of our daily hours sleeping, which means roughly eight hours each day, to give our bodies the rest they need. But truth be told, that eight-hour commitment doesn't always play out in our culture the way it should. Whether we are susceptible to internal distractions (racing thoughts, spinning anxieties, or obsessive ruminations) or external distractions (Netflix, Instagram, good novels, gaming, or YouTube), we often trade some of our most precious sleep time for momentary diversions.

In the past, before the industrial revolution and the existence of modern electricity, people went to sleep as soon as the sun went down. Not only was it harder to see after dark, but there was nothing to keep them awake. According to social psychologist Dr. James B. Maas, "Before Thomas Edison's invention of the electric light in 1879, most people slept ten hours each night, a duration we've just recently discovered is ideal for optimal performance. When activity no longer was limited by the day's natural light, sleep habits changed."[2] There's even evidence that people of ancient days used to sleep *twice*, meaning they would sleep for a few hours as soon as the sun went down, wake for a few hours to pray, to make time for intimacy, or to do something else, and then go back to sleep until the sun came up again in the morning. Their lives were dictated by circadian rhythms, responding to the cycles of dark and light.

SLEEP = TRUST

Our lives today seem to be dictated less by circadian rhythms and more by the rhythms and messages of culture: Do more, grind more, hustle more, think more, worry more, scheme more—and sleep less. But this is not the way of Jesus.

One of my favorite passages in Scripture actually has to do with sleep. Mark 4 sets the scene of Jesus and His disciples after a long day of ministry. Jesus had been teaching, preaching, and pouring out hour after hour after hour to large crowds, and He was exhausted. In a way, I can relate to this type of strain. I've been traveling and speaking and counseling for almost a decade now, yet I don't think I'll ever become immune to the emotional and physical drain of pouring out to others in this specific way. Ministering to large crowds of people for an extended period of time demands a significant expenditure. There's an expected aftermath that I refer to as the post-ministry crash, which I often say feels very similar to getting hit by a truck.

I can imagine Jesus was feeling that post-ministry crash after a long day of serving and teaching and preaching. Let's read about it directly from Mark 4:

> That day when evening came, he said to his disciples, "Let us go over to the other side." Leaving the crowd behind, they took him along, just as he was, in the boat. There were also other boats with him. A furious squall came up, and the waves broke over the boat, so that it was nearly swamped. Jesus was in the stern, sleeping on a cushion. The disciples woke him and said to him, "Teacher, don't you care if we drown?"
>
> He got up, rebuked the wind and said to the waves, "Quiet! Be still!" Then the wind died down and it was completely calm.
>
> He said to his disciples, "Why are you so afraid? Do you still have no faith?"
>
> They were terrified and asked each other, "Who is this? Even the wind and the waves obey him!" (Mark 4:35-41).

As I read this passage, three important concepts stand out that I believe would do us well to remember:

Jesus understood and honored the limitations of His body. He knew His human body had limits. Let that sink in for a minute. He was acutely aware of how His body felt. And this isn't the only time in Scripture where we see Jesus feeling exhausted. John 4:6 tells us Jesus was wearied by His journey. He was aware of His human capacity *and* His human needs. Having needs did not make Him weak, or flawed, or sinful, or lacking in faith—it made Him human. And not only did He understand the limitations of His earthly body, but He also honored those limitations by resting instead of pushing Himself. How many times do we, in our exhaustion and fatigue, judge and shame ourselves for being "weak" rather than stop to honor the capacity of our own humanity? And then, when we push ourselves even harder, we

> If Jesus Himself had to stop and honor the limitations of His body, how much more do we?

wonder why we're struggling and burned-out. If Jesus Himself had to stop and honor the limitations of His body, how much more do we?

Jesus gave Himself permission to rest. Not only did Jesus have an awareness of His capacity, He did something about it. He didn't need permission from others to stop and rest—He gave *Himself* permission to stop and rest when He needed to. He was in tune with Himself and His needs. He set the standard for His pace because no one else can be more aware of what's going on inside of us better than ourselves. Even though He knew He only had limited time to minister on this earth before He would die for our sins, and while others might be driven by urgency to minister to the people around them, He still saw the importance of taking the time to rest and gave Himself permission to do so. He stopped and paced Himself (John 4:6), took naps (Mark 4:38), and "reclined at the table" (Luke 7:36) when He needed to slow down and recharge. The best graphic t-shirt I ever saw said in big, bold letters: "Jesus Took Naps. Be More Like Jesus." I think I need to get one of those to remind myself that it's a Christlike thing to do to stop and rest.

Resting was an act of faith and trust. It's one thing to take a nap. It's another thing to take a nap in the middle of a massive storm, at the bottom of a boat that's getting smashed by waves and starting to fill up with water (Mark 4:35-41). That's some miraculous sleep right there. In contrast, I'm typically a light sleeper who can barely sleep through a drizzle of rain even if I'm in the comfort of my own bed—forget about trying to sleep on a boat that's getting thrown around amid a "furious storm" (Matthew 8:24). Jesus was next-level! He was a really good sleeper! But I wonder if part of His ability to sleep so deeply was rooted in His ability to trust God so fully. He was able to rest *in Him*. As King David puts it, "My soul finds rest in God" (Psalm 62:1). You see, sleep is also an act of faith. To sleep is like saying, "I trust God so much that I'm willing to close my eyes and rest, knowing He still holds the world and everything in it in His mighty hands." Sleep declares that I am not limitless, I am not indispensable, and I am not in control. It is a confession that I have limited capacity, energy, and ability. It is a reminder that He is God, and I am not. I can give myself permission to rest because I have faith in a God who stays awake on my behalf—a God who neither slumbers nor sleeps, so that I can (Psalm 4:8). Scripture gives us invitation after invitation to give God our burdens and truly rest: "Come to me, all you who are weary and burdened, and I will give you rest. Take my yoke upon you and learn from me, for I am gentle and humble in heart, and you will find rest for your souls" (Matthew 11:28-29). Rest for our souls. Isn't that exactly what we're looking for?

I wonder if Jesus was able to rest (both physically and emotionally) undisturbed by the chaos around Him because of the peace that resided in Him and the faith and trust He had in the God who went before Him. Psalm 139:5 says it best: "You go before me and follow me. You place your hand of blessing on my head" (NLT). What a sheer gift of trust to be able to close your eyes in sleep. As Psalm 4:8 so beautifully says, "In peace I will lie down and sleep,

> I can give myself permission to rest because I have faith in a God who stays awake on my behalf.

for you alone, LORD, make me dwell in safety." Are you able to emotionally rest in Him, allowing your body to physically rest too?

THE GIFT OF SLEEP

If you're anything like me, sleep hasn't always come easy. On the other hand, I always joke that my husband has the "spiritual gift of sleep" since he can sleep through almost anything. I kid you not: Once, on an out-of-town trip we took, an earthquake shook the entire town we were staying in, and John slept right through it. He didn't even roll over in bed. Not even a tiny flinch. Talk about a skilled sleeper. But in a way, sleep really is a gift. Psalm 127:2 says, "It is in vain that you rise up early and go late to rest, eating the bread of anxious toil; for he gives to his beloved sleep" (ESV). I love this verse, but if I'm honest, there were seasons in my life when this verse rubbed me the wrong way—specifically, when I was struggling with insomnia.

I remember times when the impending night seemed like impending doom because I knew I wouldn't be able to sleep the way I needed to. I would stay awake for hours, watching the clock tick from one hour to the next, while my mind buzzed and my restless body tossed and turned. If sleep is such a gift, why wasn't God giving it to me? The lack of sleep also impacted so many other parts of my life, including my energy the next day as well as my mood.

Looking back on those difficult seasons, I now understand my insomnia was a signal—a sign that something was off underneath the surface of my life and needed to be addressed. Whether it signaled depression and anxiety, chemical and hormonal imbalances, or unhealthy nighttime habits—something needed to change. If you are struggling with insomnia that has lasted longer than two weeks (waking up multiple times a night, lying awake for hours, ruminating over things beyond your control, or waking up too early and not being able to fall back asleep), I challenge you to see it as a signal. What do you need to address or pay attention to?

Whether it means taking care of your mental and emotional health with the help of a professional counselor,[3] dealing with past trauma that may be contributing to nightmares, getting the vitamins and supplements you need, checking on your physical health with a medical doctor and getting the proper medications, or getting into a rhythm of healthy nighttime habits, your sleep will eventually return to where it needs to be.

Here are some things you can do in the meantime to encourage better sleep hygiene:

- Avoid caffeine close to bedtime.
- Sleep and wake at the same time every day.
- Keep your room cool and dark.
- Limit screen time before bed. (The light from screens can arouse your body to wake mode.)
- Limit daytime naps to 30 minutes or less, and only take naps within the first half of your waking hours.
- Follow a similar bedtime routine each night.
- Increase your amount of daily sunshine exposure to recalibrate your circadian rhythm.

* Exercise regularly during the day.[4]

Remember that a lack of sleep is a signal of some underlying issue. We may go through seasons of insomnia, but insomnia should never be our norm. The gift of sleep is available to all of us. We just have to make it a priority.

CHOOSING SLEEP

Choosing sleep means choosing to be disciplined with how I spend my nighttime hours: putting screens away, turning off the TV, closing my laptop, and silencing my phone. It means honoring my humanity and acknowledging my limits. It means realizing that in stopping to rest and recharge, I am choosing to give God my best for the next day. The main reason so many people struggle to sleep eight hours a day is because they choose not to. In our productivity-driven world, we make idols out of efficiency and bow down to the false god of "doing more" when the God who has already done it all is beckoning us to stop and rest. To be still and know that He is God (Psalm 46:10). In choosing to stop, rest, nap, and sleep, I remind myself that He is God and I am not. I am acknowledging that He will work, fight, and act on my behalf, and even as I close my eyes to rest, the Lord will continue to fight the battles I cannot (Exodus 14:14). I am choosing to still my mind and relax my body in order to take good care of the life God has entrusted me with. If Jesus needed to choose sleep, how much more do we? Consider this your permission to stop and rest. Remember, Jesus took naps. Be more like Jesus.

> In stopping to rest and recharge, I am choosing to give God my best for the next day.

Verse for Reflection

In vain you rise early and stay up late, toiling for food to eat—
for he grants sleep to those he loves (Psalm 127:2).

Today's Rhythm: PERMISSION TO SLEEP

1. How many hours of sleep do you get each night? What, if anything, inhibits you from getting eight hours of sleep each night? List out anything that comes to mind.

2. If lack of sleep signals something is wrong underneath the surface, what might you need to address, eliminate, or change in order to get more sleep?

3. What type of things do you find your mind ruminating on or worrying about when it's time to shut down each night? What is your reaction to the idea that sleep is an act of trusting God, recognizing that He is God and you are not?

4. Consider repeating this prayer when you struggle to sleep at night: *Lord, as I close my eyes to rest, I acknowledge that You are a God who does not sleep or slumber. Right now, I give You my racing thoughts, my worried mind, my restless body, and my unresolved problems. I ask You to*

work on my behalf while I rest. I ask You to give me confidence and peace, as I believe You are fighting for me while I rest in Your mighty power and strength. In closing my eyes and choosing to sleep, I acknowledge that I trust You, and that You are Jehovah-Jireh, my Provider. Thank You for the gift of sleep. I receive it in Jesus's name. Amen.

Chapter 10

PACE YOURSELF

Rhythms of Rest

"YOU NEED TO LIVE AT 85 PERCENT."

He looked at me perplexed, as if he wasn't sure if this was the best advice he'd ever heard or the worst. But he jotted it down on the yellow lined notebook he had brought to session anyway, so I knew it had struck a chord. I was working with one of my clients, a high-capacity leader, who was recovering from a serious burnout situation that almost mentally broke him. "You can't live at 100 percent and expect to go very far. You might go fast, but you won't go far." I reiterated: "You've got to learn to live at 85 percent."

I know that doesn't sound like the typical advice you get from your parents, teachers, instructors, trainers, coaches, or maybe even pastors who tell you to give 100 percent. "Give it all you've got!" they say. For your team, for your family, for your church, for your job—give everything you've got to the very last drop. But I'm not a fan of that rhetoric, and when we misinterpret this concept, we end up doing more harm than good. Instead, living at 85 percent is my mantra as a professional counselor. It's a piece of advice I give to my clients on a regular basis.

Now, please hear me. What I'm not saying is "don't give your best." I don't mean that at all. We should always give our best and do everything as if we're doing it for the Lord (Colossians 3:23-24). What I mean is that you shouldn't live at 100 percent capacity. I think we often assume that giving our best and doing our best means living at 100 percent capacity all the time. But in fact, I would argue that giving our best actually means living at 85 percent so we have energy left over—a reserve to draw from when a need arises. If we're honest with ourselves, we can admit that always living at maximum capacity isn't healthy.

LIVE BELOW YOUR MEANS

The concept of living under capacity is a necessary principle, but we specifically hear about it in the world of budget and finance. Any financial expert will tell you that the financially wise thing to do when you get your paycheck is to live under capacity. They call it "living below your means." If you spend 100 percent of your paycheck every time you get paid, you'll have nothing left in savings. Not only will you have nothing available to cover an emergency, such as an urgent medical bill or an unexpected water heater repair, but you'll also have nothing left to give and share toward a financial need in your family, a crisis in your community, or a global tragedy. When you're living at 100 percent capacity, you have nothing with which to bless others.

Think about that concept for a moment in terms of your emotional, relational, and physical energy. Are you living at 100 percent capacity, or do you have a reserve? Is there margin in your life and in your schedule, or are you constantly maxed out? Are you going far, or are you just going fast?

JOURNEY VERSUS DESTINATION

We live in a fast-paced culture. I don't think any of us would argue with that. We want everything faster and faster, from the speed of our Wi-Fi to our drive-thru experience. We want to get to the destination

ASAP, so much so that we often forget to pay attention to the journey. But where exactly are we headed? And then what happens when we get there? What even *is* the destination? Is it to make more money? To accomplish some big goal? To get married and have kids? To buy that house?

The funny thing about destinations is that typically, once we reach them, we immediately set more new destinations for ourselves. As soon as we meet a goal, we set another one. We're chasing never-ending goals, dreams, and destinations, *and* we're missing the journey along the way.

When I look at the life of Jesus, He was a man who lived more for the journey than the destination. Rather than rushing to get to the end of things, He paced Himself. He appreciated and made the most of His time. Because for Him, the journey was about the people He met and loved. So often He was interrupted on the way from one place to the next, but because He was living with margin, He had the time to stop, have compassion, and notice people's needs—even when He was on His way to do something important (like healing a young girl who was on her deathbed). Though Jesus was often on His way somewhere, He stopped whenever someone else needed His attention. (See Luke 8:40-56, for example.) He stopped to have compassion on someone who needed Him because He didn't live life in a rush. He didn't allow the pressure of others to set His pace.

When I think of the pressure Jesus felt from others, I think about the story of Lazarus. Mary and Martha had sent word to Jesus that their brother was sick. He replied to that message by essentially saying that all would be well, because He was Jesus and He knew all things. But what happened next? Instead of rushing there, He stayed put: "Jesus loved Martha and her sister and Lazarus. So when he heard that Lazarus was sick, he stayed where he was two more days" (John 11:5-6). We don't know why Jesus did that because Scripture doesn't tell us specifically. Was it because He needed a few days to rest from the previous ministry marathon? Was it because He knew He was crossing into enemy territory and people there wanted Him dead? Or was it to make sure His power to bring life and raise the dead would be displayed if Lazarus was allowed to die? We don't know the details, but we do know that everything Jesus did was "for God's glory so that God's Son may be glorified through it" (John 11:4).

But the most crucial thing I see in this story is the affirmation that Jesus did not live by the pressure of the people around Him. He set his own pace. His own rhythm. His own cadence. We could sure learn a lot from matching His pace.

PACE YOURSELF

If you've read enough of my books by now, you'll know I'm not a runner. If you ever happen to see me running, you should probably start running too, because there's a good chance we're being chased by something ferocious and dangerous! But all jokes aside, you can learn a lot from runners. One of the main things I've learned from my friends who engage in the sport of running is the idea of pacing oneself. A runner's pace is essentially their sustainable speed—a speed that isn't too fast and isn't too slow. They have to find their pace and stick to it; it's how they manage their energy and their efforts, their rate of output throughout the run. If they ignore their pace and just choose to run as fast as they can, they will push their body too hard, spike their heart rate, struggle to breathe, run out of energy, and fail to complete the race. Like I mentioned earlier, it's the idea that you can either run fast—or you can run far. But you can't do both.

Let's consider this concept as it applies to our daily lives and routines. We have to learn to pace ourselves the way Jesus did so we can set ourselves up for success. The Christian life isn't just about going fast; it's about going far. It's about running the race of life that God has called us to with endurance (Hebrews 12:1).

I even see this concept of pace in the Old Testament. I was reading the book of Exodus, where it specifically talks about following the cloud of the Lord: "In all the travels of the Israelites, whenever the cloud lifted from above the tabernacle, they would set out; but if the cloud did not lift, they did not set out—until the day it lifted. So the cloud of the LORD was over the tabernacle by day, and fire was in the cloud by night, in the sight of all the Israelites during all their travels" (Exodus 40:36-38). God was the one who set their pace. He told them when to stop and when to go. But here's the kicker: They followed the pace. They obeyed. I don't know about you, but I think I'd be in a rush to get to my destination if I'd been living almost 40 years in the wilderness. *Let's get there already! Let's move it! Come on, people, let's do this!* But God knew it wasn't just about the destination. It was about the journey too. The character, faith, perseverance, hope, and trust in the Lord that they would develop along the way was far more significant than the destination itself. His presence was more important than the promised land (Exodus 33:14). Pursuing their godliness was far more important than pursuing their goal.

RHYTHMS OF REST

Rhythms of rest are a central theme in Scripture. But are they a central theme in our lives? Open the Bible, and it won't take you long to find a verse about the importance of stopping to rest, refraining from work, and honoring God with a weekly Sabbath. In fact, right smack-dab in the middle of the Ten Commandments in Exodus 20, somewhere in between having no false Gods and not murdering, we read about the rhythm of Sabbath rest: "Remember the Sabbath day by keeping it holy. Six days you shall labor and do all your work, but the seventh day is a sabbath to the LORD your God. On it you shall not do any work...For in six days the LORD made the heavens and the earth, the sea, and all that is in them, but he rested on the seventh day. Therefore the LORD blessed the Sabbath day and made it holy" (Exodus 20:8-11).

Six days a week are for work, but one day a week is for rest and, more specifically, for honoring God with our slow pace. I decided to approach that commandment in terms of a percentage, and guess what six days out of seven comes out to? Yep. About 85 percent (85.714286 percent, to be exact). Maybe there's something to the 85 percent concept, even deeper than what I realized. What if we were to look at our entire lives through the lens of 85 percent? In how we structure our days, our weeks, our months, and our years? What if we lived at a pace that left us with margin, space, and time to pour into our own souls, as well as into the souls of others? What if we reserved the bandwidth to do so? To me, this sounds like a glorious way to live.

What does the rhythm of rest look like in your life today? It's one thing for us to acknowledge the concept of Sabbath as a biblical idea, but it's a whole other thing to actually live it out and build a life of margin. We're going to further address the concept of margin and boundaries in upcoming chapters, but for now, I want to give you a few practical ideas for learning to pace yourself (and living at 85 percent):

- Set aside one day a week (it doesn't have to be Sunday) to slow down and invest in soul care—time with God, time with yourself, and time with others—that fills you up.

- Build pockets of time into your daily routine to pause, breathe, think, pray, slow down, and connect with God. Even just a few minutes out of an hour can go a long way for your mental and physical health.

- Analyze your weekly schedule and routines and make sure they're reflective of the *essentials*. Don't fill your time with meaningless obligations, and don't commit to things simply because you feel pressured or threatened by the pace of others. Set your own pace. What does a sustainable pace look like in your life?

- Look at your monthly schedule and make sure you have space in case an unexpected need, ministry opportunity, or chance for rest arises. Don't live at max capacity on purpose.

- Look at your yearly calendar and make sure you have times built in for regular soul care. (For example: a vacation or staycation, whether for a whole week, a few days, or even a 24-hour period.) Don't wait until you're in desperate need or on the verge of breakdown to set that time aside. Schedule your rest intentionally so the rhythms of refreshment are a routine part of your yearly cycle.

GUILT BE GONE

Something holding many people back from healthy rhythms of rest are feelings of guilt and shame. They feel bad, wrong, or lazy when they slow down and pace themselves. They've been brainwashed by the culture of go-go-go, which claims that slowing down intentionally is counterintuitive. But do you realize that slowing down is exactly what your body needs to function at its best? God gave the human body an important gift called the autonomic nervous system. This internal regulation system essentially helps the body know when to go and when to stop. One side of this system, the sympathetic nervous system, gives us the jolt of energy we need to wake up and get going, the motivation to accomplish and move, the signals to be alert and aware—while the complementary side of this system (the parasympathetic nervous system) slows down our body, helps us to achieve calm and rest, regulates our heart rate and our breathing, and shuts down our body so we can fall asleep and stay asleep. Without our parasympathetic nervous system, we'd be constantly wired and on edge. Without our sympathetic nervous system, we'd never get out of bed. We need both to function at our best.

> Slowing down is exactly what your body needs to function at its best.

Interestingly enough, when we're constantly in a hurried state, we're actually telling our sympathetic nervous system to stay on high alert all the time. We become our own worst enemy. We become the threat that puts our body into fight-or-flight mode because we're doing too much rather than balancing our body with the rhythms of rest. But you cannot live in high-alert, high-efficiency, high-productivity mode all the time without something eventually breaking down. The body's motor gets so overwhelmed and so overheated by overactivity that it eventually comes to a halt. This is what we call burnout. A guaranteed shutdown. This can happen by way of a physical shutdown (a stress-induced illness) or a mental shutdown (the onset of a mental illness such as anxiety and depression), or in some cases, both. God knows how our bodies work. He loves and cares for us so much that He built rhythms of rest into our routine. He's set the pace. The question is this: Do we trust Him enough to follow that pace? Will we submit ourselves to the speed He's modeled for us, the rhythms of rest He's gifted us, or will we try and get ahead?

I don't know about you, but I don't want to try to live in a way that outpaces God. Instead, I want to be in sync with His Spirit. I want to follow Him in His pace, and His rhythms, and His rest. Because if you ask me, that's the only place where true rest can be found.

Verse for Reflection

The LORD replied, "My Presence will go with you, and I will give you rest" (Exodus 33:14).

Today's Rhythm: RHYTHMS OF REST

1. What's your reaction to the idea of living at 85 percent? Why?

2. How would you describe the pace and rhythms of Jesus? What do your current pace and rhythms of rest look like?

3. How can you build rhythms of rest into your day? Your week? Your month? Your year? Write down your ideas.

4. Do you have any guilt or shame surrounding your ideas of rest? Where do you think those feelings began, and why? How can you begin replacing the unnecessary guilt and shame with God's pace for your life?

CONNECT

✝

Caring for Your Soul Through
Life-giving Relationships

Chapter 11

STAY CONNECTED

The Rhythm of Community

"I'VE BEEN SO HURT IN RELATIONSHIPS," SHE SAID IN one of our sessions, tears slowly building in the corners of her eyes and then escaping down her face. "Rejection is extremely hard, and for some reason, I've had more than my fair share of it." We had started meeting one-on-one because Katie was struggling in a self-made pit of isolation that had led to feelings of depression. She was feeling so far removed from the concept of relationships, much less the far-fetched idea of Christian community, that she didn't know how to begin to get back to a healthy place. All she knew was that she was battling a heavier loneliness than she had ever felt before. And 2020 didn't help. If anything, the year pushed her and so many others into more isolation than they ever thought possible. But her suffocating loneliness was her signal that something needed to change—that it was time to take risks again, to open her heart, to try again.

That's not an easy place to be when you've been hurt. You see, your brain is hardwired to protect you, to remind you of all the bad things that have happened in the past and the dangers of putting yourself out there again. It crunches the data and maps out a safety plan to keep it from happening again. Just like a child who touches a hot stove and gets a serious burn, a memory map sears into his brain so he never touches a hot stove again. Our brain wants to keep us safe. It's the primary goal. But often in keeping you "safe," it also keeps you isolated, empty, and alone. It may assess the external risk to keep your body from harm, but it doesn't always do the best job assessing the internal risk: the deprivation of your soul, the loneliness of your heart, and the isolation of your spirit.

STERILE SOULS

In a way, the social distancing movement of 2020 gave us all an excuse to do what many of us want to do deep down: stay safe. It affirmed the message that if we keep people at a distance, we'll be safer. Safe from heartbreak, safe from pain, safe from rejection, and safe from getting hurt. And on one hand, it was true. When it came to the medical implications of a lethal virus, social distancing was both necessary and wise. But years later, even with the threat of the virus subsiding, how many of us have carried that same approach into our relationships? We may feel sterile and safe in our body, but now we're also dealing with sterile and lifeless souls.

Getting hurt in relationships is a real risk. Almost all of us have had to endure relational pain at some point. But while we're avoiding the risk of hurt by staying in isolation, we're also numbing our hearts and sterilizing our souls. C.S. Lewis puts it this way in his book *The Four Loves*:

> To love at all is to be vulnerable. Love anything, and your heart will certainly be wrung and possibly be broken. If you want to make sure of keeping it intact, you must give it to no one, not even to an animal. Wrap it carefully round with hobbies and little luxuries; avoid all entanglements; lock it up safe in the casket or coffin of your selfishness. But in that casket—safe, dark, motionless, airless—it will change. It will not be broken; it will become unbreakable, impenetrable, irredeemable.[1]

We have exchanged the intimacy of vulnerability for the "safety" of loneliness. The culture of loneliness and isolation has significantly impacted our spiritual, emotional, and mental health. One-third of adults ages 45 and older report feeling lonely.[2] Loneliness has been found to contribute to both physical and mental health factors. Physically, loneliness has been found to increase the risk of mortality by up to 32 percent.[3] Meaning that loneliness can literally kill you. People who don't have friends are twice as likely to die prematurely, which is a statistic even more lethal than smoking 20 cigarettes in a day![4] We talk about the physical dangers of cigarettes all the time, but how often do we hear about the physical dangers of loneliness? Loneliness and isolation also increase the risk of depression, cognitive decline, and dementia in older adults.[5] It has even been found to have a direct impact on health factors, including blood pressure, immune functioning, and inflammation.[6]

Loneliness also impacts our mental health. People who have good friendships respond to stress better than those who don't. Studies show that people who talked to a supportive friend about a stressful event had lower blood pressure and heart rate than those who talked with someone they considered to be ambivalent.[7] Not only that, but people who have friends and who feel satisfied in their relationships are less likely to suffer from depression.[8] According to the literature, there's an astounding association between the risk of suicide and loneliness. It's an epidemic we can't afford to ignore.

THE RHYTHM OF RELATIONSHIPS

When we're talking about loneliness and isolation, what we're really talking about is a lack of social connection. Feeling disconnected from the people around you. Feeling separated from a community.

The irony isn't lost on me that we're investing more time than ever as a nation trying to "connect" on social media, yet despite the astronomical number of hours we spend online, we

> We were made to connect with real people in real ways.

feel more disconnected than ever before. Something is clearly not working. We were made to connect with real people in real ways. It's not only important for our physical and mental health, but it's also necessary for us to have healthy souls.

IT'S NOT OPTIONAL

Being social isn't optional. It's required.

It's a prerequisite to being a healthy person. When we look at the psychological components to health and well-being, connection to others is crucial to a thriving, well-adjusted, meaningful life. In fact, the opposite of that—isolation—is the very thing used to punish, torture, and wreak havoc on the human mind and body. In the prison system, even though only upward of 8 percent of people are sent to solitary confinement, half the people who die by suicide within the penal system are the ones placed in solitary confinement.[9] Not only that, but those who were exposed to solitary confinement had a higher likelihood of dying by suicide after their release.[10] Yet somehow, in the wake of our hurts, we continue to believe that loneliness, isolation, and withdrawal are somehow the safer option.

Community is a biblical reality in addition to a psychological necessity. Whether you consider yourself an introvert, extrovert, or omnivert, understanding and engaging in community is an important part of being a healthy person as well as an important part of being a Christian. Scripture consistently talks about the value of community. In fact, right at the start of the unfolding story, we read ten powerful words out of the mouth of God in Genesis 2:18: "The LORD God said, 'It is not good for the man to be alone.'" And so He created us, in His image, to live and breathe and move in the context of community.

- Psalm 133:1: "How good and pleasant it is when God's people live together in unity!"
- Hebrews 10:24-25: "Let us consider how we may spur one another on toward love and good deeds, not giving up meeting together, as some are in the habit of doing, but

encouraging one another—and all the more as you see the Day approaching."

* Galatians 6:2: "Carry each other's burdens, and in this way you will fulfill the law of Christ."

* Romans 12:4-5: "For just as each of us has one body with many members, and these members do not all have the same function, so in Christ we, though many, form one body, and each member belongs to all the others."

* 1 Corinthians 12:13: "For we were all baptized by one Spirit so as to form one body."

* Ephesians 4:2-4: "Make every effort to keep the unity of the Spirit through the bond of peace. There is one body and one Spirit, just as you were called to one hope when you were called."

* Acts 2:44-47: "All the believers were together and had everything in common. They sold property and possessions to give to anyone who had need. Every day they continued to meet together in the temple courts. They broke bread in their homes and ate together with glad and sincere hearts, praising God and enjoying the favor of all the people. And the Lord added to their number daily those who were being saved."

Jesus Himself understood these truths, and He was deliberate in His pursuit of community. He surrounded Himself with and entrusted Himself to a community of friends and family—His inner circle. He prioritized the give-and-take of life-giving relationships. In fact, for three whole years, He lived in community with His disciples. They traveled together, ate together, told stories together, served together, prayed together, and even shared their finances. They did life together. All of life. The ups and downs. The good and bad. The humorous and hard. They lived in community with one another. The Greek word for this is *koinonia*—the idea of fellowship with others. It comes from the word *koinonos*, which means partner, sharer, or companion. According to writer Jessica Brodie, "Koinonia is more than friendship. It is a divinely intimate, holy unity among believers—and between believers and the Lord—involving everything from spiritual oneness in the Holy Spirit, community life, sharing contributions from money to food to gifts, and the communion partaken in the body and blood of Christ Jesus."[11]

I think this is something we're missing, specifically in our Western society. We mostly do life alone, and at best, we come together every now and again. But what about cultivating a community? People who choose to do life together?

DOING LIFE TOGETHER

When I look back at different stages of my life, community has always been a big part of them. But I can confidently say that community is never something that has "just happened." Not once. It's always been something I've had to make happen. Just like any other area of discipline in my life, community had to be a priority. Community is one way I make sure to care for my soul. I've had to be deliberate and intentional in initiating friendships, extending invitations, practicing vulnerability, asking for help with my needs, and inviting people into both my home and my heart.

Just like I am the initiator of the health of my body, prioritizing nutrition, hydration, and movement, I've had to be the initiator of the health of my social life as well. I want to take responsibility for my social health because I'm the one who suffers most from the effects of isolation and loneliness when I don't. I'm the one who ends up living with a sterile soul rather than a satisfied soul! Inspired by the life of Jesus, by the way He did community, and by my experience as a professional counselor, I've noted a few things to consider when cultivating a rhythm of community and connection:

Deal with Your Hurts: If past hurts are holding you back, that's glaring evidence that you need to deal with your hurts first. You won't be able to establish new, healthy relationships if you're still defaulting to a past template of unhealthy connection. I would encourage you to consider a season of counseling, which may help you identify how to set boundaries, protect your heart, become healthy standing alone, and distinguish healthy relationships from unhealthy relationships. Get in tune with your role in relationships and what you can do to add to the health of the relationships you find yourself in. I always tell people that the healthier you become emotionally, the easier it is to recognize relationships that are good for you. You may have had a few really bad experiences, and for that, I'm deeply sorry—but don't allow those experiences to become your pattern. Don't allow those experiences to deter you from the life-giving relationships you were meant to have. Rewrite the story by healing, growing, and then trying again.

> The healthier you become emotionally, the easier it is to recognize relationships that are good for you.

Get Plugged In: I can tell you what definitely doesn't work in cultivating community: doing nothing. So many people are lonely and isolated because they're waiting for people to cultivate community with them rather than initiating community themselves. When I look at the relationships that Jesus modeled (which we'll examine more in the next chapter), one of my primary takeaways is that He was intentional. He didn't wait for relationships to happen; He made them happen. He cultivated them. Look around right now and ask yourself if you're being purposeful in your social life. Are you actively serving and connecting in your church? Is there a ministry or service opportunity you could get plugged in with? Does your church offer life groups, small groups, or community groups with which you can get involved? Do you have a hobby or interest that puts you in closer proximity to others? Push yourself out of your comfort zone and connect.

My relational life has been littered with ministry groups, small groups, church groups, mission trips, and even neighborhood groups. And when there was no group to join and no one who seemed interested, I started something myself and invited as many people as I knew to join me. And in every season of my life, as I have been deliberate in pursuing my people, God has blessed me with rich and meaningful friendships. It didn't happen overnight, but it always happened eventually. Sometimes friendships would come into my life for a while, and other friendships have lasted a lifetime—but in both situations, I have found a community of people who have stretched me, challenged me, and shaped me into the person I am today. But I had to be the one to care for the health of my soul by pursuing healthy community.

Look for Give-and-Take: Healthy relationships are defined by give-and-take. This is an important piece to the puzzle, and a key component in cultivating community. Some people are wired to give, give, and give without expecting anything from anyone in return. But that doesn't lead to a life of community; it leads to a life of burnout and one-sided relationships. When it comes to establishing community, you want to be a person who is both giving and receiving, on the lookout for people who are both giving and receiving. Healthy relationships are a two-way street—they must be if you want them to last. If you find yourself in a relationship where you're doing most or all of the work, confront that dynamic! And if confronting it doesn't change it, slowly distance yourself from that person, decrease your expectations of them, and then begin looking for and investing in relationships where there's a healthier pattern of exchange. Jesus was so good at giving, but believe it or not, He also asked for things in return. He asked His friends for help and shared His needs with them. Even though He was God, He knew that healthy relationships were defined by give-and-take, and He gave His friends the opportunity to give back to Him both emotionally and physically (Luke 22:8).

Invite People In: If healthy community is defined by what Jesus and His disciples modeled, what could a modern version of that look like in our world? I mean, I'm not going to live in a commune or anything of the sort, but what does it look like to purposely let people into my life and into my heart? To me, it looks like being purposeful with my calendar and making sure the people who mean the most to me have priority with my time. It means making sure to connect with, check in with, and keep in touch with "my people" on a regular (even daily) basis. It means opening my home, even when it's a mess, and pulling up chairs to the table so we can sit down together and share a meal. Sometimes it's a fancy home-cooked meal, and other times it's leftovers. But in either case, the community matters more than the commodities. Building community means sharing the highs and lows of my life, opening up about my strengths and weaknesses, and asking for prayer or practical help when I have a need. It means talking about what God is doing in our lives, what we're learning, and where we're struggling. It means doing life together when life is beautiful *and* when it's messy. Community means an open door to my home, but mostly, it's an open door to my heart.

Find a Mentor and a Disciple: The last thing I'll say about community is that it's often multilayered and multirelational. What I mean is that while most of our community will be give-and-take peer relationships, some of the community God calls us to will look a little different. Sometimes God calls us to invest in people who aren't always "giving back" in the context of a discipleship relationship, just as Jesus poured into His disciples. I think the problem for many Christians especially is that they eventually find almost *all* of their relationships looking like discipleship relationships. This is where we really must be careful, because having too many one-sided relationships paves the road to burnout, depletion, and depression.

Discipleship relationships are so important, but we must be in tune to the people God has called us to disciple as well as the people He has *not* called us to disciple. Jesus was very intentional with a small group, because He was limited by His humanity and the natural boundaries of 24 hours in day. We must also be considerate of our time, energy, and margin so we can pour out effectively to the people God has called us to disciple. Tonight, I get the privilege and honor of spending my time with the group of counselors I've committed to discipling through our monthly team meeting. One of the reasons I started the Debra Fileta Counselors Network[12] was to have an opportunity to work with counselors who are pouring hope and healing into others in the same ways so many others have poured into me and helped me become the counselor I am today.

Not only that, but we also need to be purposeful with whom we're asking and inviting to disciple us! As we're pouring out to others, we need people who can mentor us as well. I talk about this concept a lot because mentorship has been invaluable in my life. Find a mentor whom you admire, someone who is about five or ten years ahead of where you want to be both spiritually and relationally. I meet with my mentors on a regular basis and ask for advice, pick their brains, receive prayer, and glean wisdom from their life experiences.

Fittingly, before I am scheduled to meet with my team later this evening, this afternoon I have a mentorship call planned with my own spiritual mentor, Christine Caine. I can't wait to get her advice and invite her to speak into my life. I had to take a leap of faith one day many years ago in asking her to mentor me. Truth be told, it's never easy or comfortable to ask something of someone, but in the case of mentorship, it's worth it! We need to ask and allow others to invest in us. I've sought out many mentors along the way for specific reasons so I could learn as much as I could from those who have gone ahead. I had mentors as a college student, when I was dating and wanted to learn about healthy marriage, as a brand-new counselor, as a new mom, as a woman in ministry, and as a business owner. In each season of my life, I've found someone who has gone ahead of me, and specifically asked them to come alongside me on this journey. They've poured into me as I pour into others. This is the beauty of multi-relational, multigenerational community!

RHYTHMS OF COMMUNITY

Remember Katie from the beginning of this chapter? Her loneliness told her it was time to make a change. That's when she started seeing me. She decided it was finally time to deal with some of those hurts from the past, the wounds of rejection that were still lingering and keeping her soul sterile. In counseling, we worked on healing those hurts, getting her relationship anxiety under control, and helping her become emotionally healthy. And then we started rewriting the story of her experience with relationships by doing things differently. Little by little, she ventured outside of her comfort zone. Little by little, she risked opening her heart up again to the right people, in the right ways. Little by little, she began to distinguish healthy relationships from not-so-healthy ones. She took the first steps by attending a new church. Awhile later, she joined a church small group. Eventually, she found her way to a few community meetups, singles groups, and gatherings. She also started initiating one-on-one get-togethers, developing friendships, and opening up to the idea of community.

Katie has started taking control of her social and relational health, even when the insecurities and fears creep back in. She's learned that no one is perfect, but there are healthy and unhealthy rhythms to community, and she's learning how to recognize them. I'm so proud of the progress she's made, and I love seeing the way it's enriched her life, built up her confidence, and exposed areas that needed healing. God is using community to shape her, stretch her, and challenge her…but He's also using community to bless her, fill her, and heal her. And she would wholeheartedly agree.

Healthy community is a marker of a healthy soul. In contrast, isolation and loneliness are the markers of a hurting soul. In community, we learn the give-and-take of healthy relationships. Like Bob Goff says so well, "What I've come to realize is if I really want to 'meet Jesus,' then I have to get a lot closer to the people He created."[13] God Himself said it's not good to do life alone. Research backs that up. It's time for you to take ownership of the health of your soul by acknowledging the health of your community.

Verse for Reflection

The LORD *God said, "It is not good for the man to be alone" (Genesis 2:18).*

Today's Rhythm: **THE RHYTHM OF COMMUNITY**

1. On a scale of zero to ten (ten being you're immersed in a healthy community, zero being you're struggling with isolation and loneliness), what number would you give your social and relational health in this season of life?

2. Has any hurt from the past kept you from investing in healthy community? How have those hurts impacted your beliefs about relationships?

3. Have your relationships been defined by give-and-take? Why or why not?

4. What practical steps can you take toward developing a healthy community in this season? How could you open your home and open your heart to fight isolation and loneliness? (For example: hosting a small group gathering; inviting some friends over for a backyard firepit and s'mores; planning a supper club meetup; inviting some people to church and to lunch afterward; getting involved in a new activity, ministry, or hobby; asking a friend for prayer or sharing a specific need; initiating a regularly scheduled hangout to put in the calendar, etc.)

Chapter 12

BE A GOOD FRIEND, HAVE A GOOD FRIEND

The Rhythm of Friendship

HAVE YOU SEEN THOSE T-SHIRTS THAT WERE GOING around a few years ago (or was it decades ago?) with the phrase "Jesus Is My Homeboy" across the front of them? I recently saw someone wearing a similar version that read "Jesus Is My BFF." I wonder if the shirts were so popular at the time because they described Jesus in a unique way: as a friend. Traditionally, we've seen God as Father and Jesus as Savior, so to see Jesus as friend provided a shift in perspective we could all use.

Have you ever thought about Jesus as a friend? Not just a "what a friend we have in Jesus" kind of friend, but a real-life, one-on-one kind of friend. Not only was Jesus a friend, but He was a really good friend. If Jesus lived in the twenty-first century, He'd probably be that friend who sends text emojis and gifs at the end of the night just to make you laugh before bed. He'd be the friend who calls the rest of the group with plans for where to meet up for dinner. He'd be the one inviting Himself over to your house because He misses you and wants to hang out. (See Luke 19:5 if you're not convinced.) He'd be the friend who's always telling you how much you mean to Him and how glad He is to have you in His life. He'd be the one FaceTiming—probably a group call, too, which wouldn't feel awkward to Him—because He just wants to check in, see everyone's face, and hear what everyone's been up to today. He'd be the friend who texts you those long voice recordings because He cares less about how His voice sounds and more about how you are doing. He'd be the friend to show up when you're struggling or having a bad day, and you would know without a shadow of a doubt that He's going to pray for you consistently and passionately, even if it means He has to stay up all night. (See John 17.) Jesus was such a good friend. As I look at the life of Jesus in Scripture, and specifically His rhythms in friendship, a few things stand out to me that I believe we could learn a lot from today. Jesus Himself showed us how to care for our souls as well as the souls of the people God has placed in our lives—namely, our friends.

Be Purposeful: Jesus was purposeful with His friendships, having literally chosen His friends (John 15:16). He had a clear reason for choosing the people He invited into His life. He didn't haphazardly default to whoever was around or whoever was the most convenient. He actually spent an entire night praying about it, asking God for guidance before He chose the people He would call His friends (Luke 6:12-13). How purposeful and deliberate are you with the people you bring into your life? Do you base your friendships on whoever happens to be in proximity, or do you base your friendships on purpose? Do you choose friends who are convenient, or friends you feel God has called you to? It would do us well to spend some time asking God whom He wants us to commit to in our closest friendships. Because the people we surround ourselves with are the people who will rub off on us most, and vice versa. Friendships shape and influence you, so don't take your company lightly. Choose your friendships with purpose.

Be Intentional: Once Jesus chose His friends, He maintained those friendships and invested in the people He chose! He determined who His inner circle was and then committed to them. They were His people, and they knew it (John 3:22). All throughout the New Testament, we see Jesus and His friends *together* (Luke 8:1-3). He made it a point to visit His friends in their homes and spend time with them (Matthew 8:14-16; Luke 10:38-42; John 12:1-2). With intention, He made time for and connected with the people He loved, even when that meant traveling long distances and giving up His time. Because friendships aren't just found; they're formed. We must care for and maintain our friendships by investing our time, our energy, and our resources. Once you identify your core group, you've got to be intentional and loyal. Are you purposeful with your friendships? Do you invest in keeping your friendships healthy, connected, and strong? Would your friends agree or disagree?

> Friendships aren't just found; they're formed.

Be Available: Jesus made Himself available to His friends. Not only were they together often, but they could count on Him when there was a need. When Martha and Mary were worried about their sick brother, they sent word to Jesus and knew He would come to their aid (John 11:1-4). When Peter's mother-in-law was sick, Jesus was there in their time of need (Luke 4:38-39). Even when He was in a large crowd, He made Himself available to His core group by turning His attention to them alone. He had meals with them, invested in them, and shared His heart with them (John 13). Despite everything He had going on, and despite His limited time here on earth, He was never too busy for His friends. He was available for them, and He wanted them to be available for Him as well (Matthew 26:40). Because true friendship is a two-way street. Are you there for your friends? Do they know they can count on you when a need arises? When needed, can you simply be present for them?

Be Honest: True friends don't just tell you what you want to hear. They tell you what you need to hear—when it's uncomfortable, when it's awkward, and even when it might hurt. They call you higher and see the best in you. Jesus was a truth teller. He was committed to leaving His friends better than when He found them. He constantly pointed them to the truth of the Word of God, but He also lifted them up and told them the truth about who they were, what they were doing, and how they could do it better (John 13:8; Matthew 26:34; John 13:21). Are you honest with your friends? Are you able to point them to the truth of the Word of God when they are struggling to believe? Are you able to be honest, speaking the truth in love when you've been hurt, when you identify an area of struggle, or when you see something that needs to be changed? Do you create a safe and welcoming space for your friends to be honest with you? How well do you receive feedback from the people you love?

Be in Prayer: One of the most powerful things you can do for your friends is to pray for them. Jesus took the time to earnestly pray for His friends (John 17:6-26). He bridged the gap between heaven and earth on their behalf. He prayed for their protection, for their unity, and for their sanctification. He prayed for them to believe in truth, and to remain in the truth. Just like Jesus, I want to be a person who prays earnestly for my friends! I want them to know they can come to me whenever they have a need, and count on me to bring it before the throne of God! I want to be a friend who prays for my friends before they even ask—because it truly is the most powerful thing I can do for them. Do you pray for your friends? I know it's so easy to say, "I'll pray for you!" whenever someone asks for prayer. But do you actually do it? Do you commit to it? In what ways can you commit to praying for your friends the way Jesus did for His? On the other hand, how can you ask your friends to pray for you?

Be Gracious: True friendship understands that no one is perfect and gives grace and forgiveness at the proper time. I don't know about you, but considering the number of times the disciples misunderstood, wronged, and even betrayed Jesus, it would have been hard for me to offer grace. But Jesus did. Specifically, even when Peter betrayed Jesus three times, Jesus chose reconciliation. He forgave Peter and chose to rebuild trust in him again because He knew Peter's heart, his calling, and his love for Him (Matthew 16:18). When it comes to dealing with pain in friendships, we need hearts that are ready to forgive; but also, we need the wisdom to look for true repentance. Just as Jesus knew that Peter was committed to change (as evidenced by his unwavering loyalty and commitment from that point on), we also need to give grace—determining not to define our friends by their mistakes.

What I'm not talking about here is a consistent pattern of hurtful behaviors and a lack of repentance. Those types of interactions don't define a true friendship; they define a toxic one. True friendship confronts, deals with, and then moves past wrongs instead of holding grudges forevermore (Proverbs 19:11). First Corinthians 13:5 tells us that true love "keeps no record of wrongs." That doesn't mean we ignore wrongs; it just means we face them, heal from them, and then move past them. Jesus was especially good at confronting wrongs and then offering forgiveness and grace to His friends. What does it look like for us to forgive in a similar fashion? How can we be honest with our hurts, then look at our friends through the lens of grace?

Be a Servant: I grew up with a mom who embodies the term *servant-hearted*. She loves to serve and give and do for others, especially the ones she loves. And while I appreciate and adore this about her, if I'm honest, growing up with a mom who served me tirelessly led to me getting used to being served!

To be frank, serving doesn't come naturally for me—especially when it comes to any type of physically draining work. Jesus humbly displayed a servant's heart by washing His disciples' feet in John 13 and, well…I'm going to have to really dig deep here. Pair the labor of washing with the one and only body part I have a really hard time with (feet truly gross me out), and you know I'll be trying desperately to find a way out of this one!

Thankfully, for people like me, there are so many ways to serve the people you love. I have learned that serving is less about what you do and more about fostering a heart that's willing and ready to bless others. I personally love to care for people by offering emotional support, by coming alongside them in their time of need, by having meaningful conversations, by praying with them and for them, and by offering advice and encouragement. I love to cook for people, to host them in my home, and to make them feel loved, welcomed, and cherished. The key is being aware of what you have to offer, and then using those gifts, talents, and resources to bless the people around you and willingly meet their needs.

But, truth be told, serving the ones you love won't always be easy and it won't always be comfortable. Sometimes I have to serve people in ways I would rather not because it's the way they *need* to be served. Like picking up a friend who ran out of gas, babysitting a few extra kids when my house is already chaotic, giving a ride to the airport, dropping off a meal when someone is sick, or taking time out of a busy day to support a friend. Authentic friendship requires a heart of service and a spirit of selflessness. And serving always requires a level of sacrifice. I'm thankful for a God who modeled this type of love by making Himself a servant, and ultimately laying down His life for me and for you (Philippians 2). "Greater love has no one than this: to lay down one's life for one's friends" (John 15:13). In what ways can you model that heart of service and sacrifice for your friends?

> Serving is less about what you do and more about fostering a heart that's willing and ready to bless others.

There's a rhythm to relationships and a rhythm to healthy friendships. And if we truly want to fight loneliness and isolation and pursue connection, we've got to integrate these rhythms into our lives with the people God has called us to. Just like Jesus, we must be purposeful and intentional in the friendships we're forming and commit to the process. True friendship doesn't happen overnight. And sometimes, friendships come in and out of our lives in different seasons for different reasons. But the key is for us to take inventory of the relationships we're developing, and to make sure we're engaging in the give-and-take of healthy friendship. A huge part of taking care of your soul is to have a good friend and be a good friend.

Verses for Reflection

Love one another. As I have loved you, so you must love one another. By this everyone will know that you are my disciples, if you love one another (John 13:34-35).

Today's Rhythm: THE RHYTHM OF FRIENDSHIP

1. List the names of people who are currently in your core group of friends. If you don't currently have a core group, think of one or two people you would like to be purposeful in the process of forming a friendship with.

2. Out of the seven rhythms of relationships (be purposeful, be intentional, be available, be honest, be in prayer, be gracious, be a servant), which of these areas are you doing well, and which of these areas do you need to work on within your friendships?

3. Write out some ways you can commit to forming healthier, stronger, and more intentional friendships this coming year.

4. On the other hand, is there any unhealthy friendship in your life, created out of convenience, in which you feel God asking you to create distance and space? Why is this friendship unhealthy, and how can you begin to love from a distance?

PROTECT

Caring for Your Soul with Boundaries
that Protect Your Calling

Chapter 13

JESUS LOVES BOUNDARIES

Protect Your Heart

WHAT DID YOU LEARN ABOUT BOUNDARIES WHEN YOU were growing up?

I asked that question on my Instagram[1] account recently, and the answers I got were both deeply telling and deeply disturbing. Here's how people responded:

"What boundaries? I was taught to say yes to everything!"

"I was told that boundaries were not Christlike."

"I wasn't allowed to have boundaries. When I tried, people would get mad at me and shame me."

"I learned that loving someone meant you let them cross your boundaries."

"We were taught that boundaries were un-Christian."

"I was taught to respect others' boundaries, but not to develop my own."

"I was taught you couldn't have boundaries with family members."

"I was taught that boundaries were selfish and mean."

"We never talked about boundaries growing up."

"I'm in my thirties, and I'm just now learning about boundaries for the very first time."

Most answers followed the same idea: *Boundaries are harmful. Boundaries are selfish. Boundaries are nonexistent.* Now you see what I mean by deeply telling and deeply disturbing. Many people have been taught to believe that boundaries are—in and of themselves—wrong, selfish, mean, or not Christlike. I've had my fair share of interactions with people who believed this to be true. I'll never forget one conversation I had with a young man who said to me, "Boundaries are not a Christian concept. Jesus didn't have boundaries; He was focused on meeting the needs of others no matter the cost." That, my friends, couldn't be further from the truth. So, allow me to make this really clear, right here at the start of this important section:

> Boundaries are not selfish.
> Boundaries are not anti-Christian.
> Boundaries are not mean.
> Boundaries are essential to your emotional and relational health.
> Boundaries are protection.
> They protect you, your marriage, your family, and God's calling on your life.
> The most unsafe people are the people who have no boundaries.

Jesus knew the importance of boundaries, and He modeled to us how to protect what mattered. I would venture to say that Jesus loves boundaries, because boundaries protect the things that are close to God's heart.

PROTECT WHAT MATTERS

What does it mean to have healthy boundaries? Boundaries are the lines of protection we draw around our lives, keeping the valuable and meaningful things in and the distractions and excess out. Boundaries are the fence you build around your home to keep you and your people safe from harm. Boundaries determine what you will and won't allow in your life. They're the invisible guardrails that you build around the things that matter most to you.

Proverbs 4:23 talks about boundaries when it says, "Above all else, guard your heart, for everything you do flows from it." Who is responsible for guarding your heart? You are. You and you alone are put in charge of protecting your heart, because the condition of your heart impacts the condition of your life. Your heart is valuable, and it's worth protecting. And you protect your heart when you live a life with boundaries.

> Boundaries are the fence you build around your home to keep you and your people safe from harm.

Boundaries have a biblical basis. When God placed Adam and Eve in the garden, He set a boundary of protection for them by letting them know to stay away from the specific tree that would harm them. "The LORD God commanded the man, 'You are free to eat from any tree in the garden; but you must not eat from the tree of the knowledge of good and evil, for when you eat from it you will certainly die'" (Genesis 2:16-17). Boundaries keep us safe. In this case, God was setting a clear boundary to protect His children from the very thing He knew could harm them. Without boundaries, we're unsafe. In fact, not only are people who lack boundaries unsafe and unprotected, but they also become unsafe to you and others—because if they don't have boundaries with themselves, they won't have boundaries with you either. If they don't know how to protect their hearts, they won't know how to protect yours. If they can't honor their own boundaries, they certainly won't honor yours. Boundaries protect what matters!

JESUS PROTECTED HIS HEART

Jesus understood the importance of boundaries and the significance of protecting what mattered most. First and foremost, He protected His relationship with the Father. Time and time again in Scripture, we see Jesus pulling away,

> The condition of your heart impacts the condition of your life.

saying no to the obligations of life in order to say yes to obeying the Father. In Luke 5:16 we read: "Jesus often withdrew to lonely places and prayed." He *often* withdrew. He *frequently* set a boundary. He *regularly* went away, alone, to be with the Father. He knew that in order to pour out, He had to be filled up.

What makes this concept even more significant to me is the verse that comes before: "Yet the news about him spread all the more, so that crowds of people came to hear him and to be healed of their sicknesses" (Luke 5:15). Jesus was in high demand! Crowds of people were coming from all over, traveling for days and days on foot, just to be in His presence. They were longing for healing and hope! Jesus was everything they needed! And yet, what did Jesus do in response? He went away, alone, to pray. The more He was needed, the more He needed to fill up. Talk about healthy boundaries!

What I don't see in this passage is a person who spread Himself too thin, depleted Himself to the point of burnout, and met the needs of others no matter the cost. What I do see is a man who understood, though He was fully God and fully man, that He had a human capacity. He honored the limitations of His human body by taking time to be filled up by the Father. The greater the demands, the more important it was for Him to protect His heart by filling up on the only One who could really satisfy. In order to say yes to the Father, He had to say no to the demands and expectations of others. He chose obedience over obligation.

PROTECTING YOUR HEART

What do you do when the demands of life begin to stack up? What do you find yourself saying yes to out of perceived obligation, and at what expense? How often do you set boundaries around your heart to keep yourself filled and fueled? Because everything you do, the entirety of your life, flows out of the health of your heart—or lack thereof.

Growing up, my dad used to tell me that human beings are like wells. If we keep giving and giving out of our limited amount of water, we will eventually run dry. All we'll have left to give is the junk at the bottom of the well when the water runs out. I know so many people who give out of obligation and end up with a heart laced with bitterness, resentment, apathy, and irritability. And somehow, we convince ourselves that's an effective way to give—as if it's better to give out of bitterness than to not give at all. But that's completely backward to what God asks of us. He wants us to give from a healthy heart, a willing heart, a full heart, a cheerful heart. Second Corinthians 9:7 says it like this: "You must each decide in your heart how much to give. And don't give reluctantly or in response to pressure. 'For God loves a person who gives cheerfully'" (NLT). And we can only do that when we've protected our heart. When we've set boundaries around our life to allow us to give the best of who we are. Let me talk you through a few practical areas where you can begin assessing your boundaries:

Protect Your Time: What would I learn about you if I looked at your schedule? Where does most of your time go? Are you making daily space for the presence and power of the Holy Spirit, or are you filling your days with obligations and demands? Life is so full of noise, which is why finding time to be alone with God is necessary to a healthy soul. Tune out what's going on around you so you can tune in to what God is doing inside of you. If we really examine where our minutes are spent, we'll often find unnecessary things trumping the essentials, and good things taking the place of what's best. How can you begin prioritizing what matters most? How can you become the protector of your time by saying no to obligations and yes to obedience?

Protect Your Emotions: Jesus spent time pouring His heart out to the Father. He shared with God what was on His mind and heart, even amid the most difficult hours of His life (Luke 22:42; 23:34). He shared His emotions with God on a regular basis, and allowed the Father to be His first point of contact when something significant was going on. He processed, out loud, with the Father. When it comes to difficult emotions, we tend to go to everyone else but God. Sometimes, we even go to people who can't be trusted with our feelings. Jesus knew that not everyone could be trusted, so He chose to carefully steward His emotions (John 2:23-25). Be careful who you share your heart with. Don't waste your heart on people who don't appreciate it. Don't give the deepest parts of yourself to people who haven't proven they can be trusted with them (Matthew 7:6). Remember, trust isn't something you just give away; trust is something that should be earned. Go to the Father first, and then find a few people you can trust with your heart because they've proven themselves trustworthy.

Protect Your Energy: If your plate feels too full, there's a good chance it is. If you feel spread too thin, there's a good chance you are. It's important to listen to your body and understand that you have a limited amount of both emotional and physical energy each day. Not everything and everyone demanding your attention and energy should get it. It's not physiologically possible. This is why it's crucial to discern what's most essential, as well as what God has called you to, so you can begin to confidently say no to anything that doesn't fall into those categories. We'll talk more about protecting your calling in the next chapter, but for now, take inventory of your energy levels and where they're getting spent. Begin setting boundaries around your precious energy.

> We need to set boundaries around our life to allow us to give the best of who we are.

Jesus knew that in order to do all God had called Him to do, and in order to be the most effective He could be with the limited time and energy He had, He had to protect His heart and set boundaries. He knew the importance of being alone with God so He could then fill up and pour out. Are you living on empty and trying to function day in, day out, on your own strength? Or are you setting aside time to be filled by His Spirit and strength? Because nothing and no one in this world will ever be able to give you what you need—*but Him*. Make time for what matters most. Make time to fill up.

Verse for Reflection
Jesus often withdrew to lonely places and prayed (Luke 5:16).

Today's Rhythm: **PROTECT YOUR HEART**

1. As you were growing up, what did you learn or see modeled about the concept of boundaries? How did that model influence your beliefs and habits?

2. When it comes to protecting your heart, which area do you tend to struggle with: boundaries with your time, boundaries with your emotions, or boundaries with your energy?

3. Give examples of things you have a tendency to do out of obligation rather than obedience to the Father.

4. What are some ways you can begin to set boundaries in order to make space for God's Spirit and strength in your day-to-day life? What do you need to eliminate in order to make time for daily connection with God through prayer, worship, and His Word?

Chapter 14

GOD > MAN

Protect Your Calling

DID YOU KNOW THAT YOUR BODY SENDS A RUSH OF dopamine to your brain every time you get a like, a follow, or a new friend request on social media? Who knew those little hearts on Instagram had so much power? But those small affirmations trigger the body's reward system into releasing a chemical that literally makes us feel good. It's called the dopamine loop, and it's a feel-good chemical rush that's released to your brain. It's the same kind of rush you feel during sex, gambling, or any other pleasurable activity, and it's why these things have such an addicting nature. We have a generation of people who are literally addicted to our devices because of the rush of dopamine we get whenever the phone buzzes. We've become people who compulsively check our phones all throughout the day, picking them up automatically, without thought or reason—opening apps, scrolling mindlessly, searching for affirmation, looking for feedback, and seeking out that next dopamine rush.

But why do we care so much about what people think? Why are we so addicted to people-pleasing and getting the approval of strangers? Why is a like, a heart, a DM, a comment, or a thumbs-up from a random person so meaningful that it sends our body into reward mode? We are a people wired for affirmation. Wired to be known. Wired to be loved. Wired to be noticed. Additionally, we carry pain from past abandonment wounds, broken relationships, and deep rejections. We're looking for love to make us feel better. The problem is, we end up looking for love in all the wrong places.

GOD > MAN

I don't think the solution to our people-pleasing tendencies is to try not to care about people and their opinions, but rather to care about what God thinks of us more. It's not that Jesus didn't care about others; He just loved God more. We can't set healthy boundaries in our lives when we're continuously focused on the measuring stick of others' approval. We can't speak truth when our goal is to people-please. We can't honor our capacity and our calling when our primary goal is to make people happy. We have to care more about God's calling on our lives than we do about what people are calling us to do. Jesus modeled this so well that He had a reputation for pleasing God more than pleasing man. People came to Him with their questions knowing He would not bend or sway in His answers just to make them happy. They said to Him: "Teacher, we know that you are true and do not care about anyone's opinion. For you are not swayed by appearances, but truly teach the way of God" (Mark 12:14 esv).

> We have to care more about God's calling on our lives than we do about what people are calling us to do.

Jesus was able to speak the truth and have clear direction and instinctive decision-making because He prioritized God's Word above all else. He was able to protect the calling God had on His life, to be a truth teller, and ultimately to become the Savior of this world because His heart was set on pleasing God and God alone. I love how the Good News Translation puts it in Proverbs 29:25: "It is dangerous to be concerned with what others think of you, but if you trust the LORD, you are safe." It's dangerous to be concerned with others' opinions because they draw you into the path of obligation. Their demands move you, step-by-step, in the direction of a people-pleasing, boundaryless life and away from the heart and calling of God. When your goal is to make everyone happy, to be liked by all, and to be affirmed by those around you, you're no longer chasing after that which brings glory to God, but instead what brings glory to self. And you can't do both of those things at the same time. You must choose one or the other.

But on the flip side, when you care more about what God has called you to than what people think of you, setting boundaries and limits becomes routine. Protecting what God has called you to becomes the norm—no matter who does or doesn't agree with you.

PROTECTING YOUR CALLING

So what does it look like to set boundaries around what God has called you to? What does it mean for us to say *yes* to God's calling on our lives and *no* to all the other demands that come our way? This isn't a simple question, and there aren't any cookie-cutter ways to decide what matters most and what God has called us to. But as I've done some soul-searching myself, and helped many other clients navigate the concept of protective boundaries, here are a few takeaways that I hope will help you as well:

Know Who You Are and Recognize Your Unique Giftings: One crucial aspect of knowing what God has called you to is knowing who you are. When you know who you are, you better understand what types of things match your life and calling, and what types of things don't. Jesus modeled this so well. He understood His identity so clearly. He had a vision for who He was and where He was going, and nothing and no one could stop Him from doing what God had called Him to do.

Knowing your identity, your skills, your strengths, and your talents can help you identify where you're supposed to be. God made you with a unique personality and unique experiences that contribute to your unique calling. I often liken it to putting a puzzle together. Knowing yourself and recognizing your giftings is essentially like understanding your shape in the big picture of the puzzle of life. The more you know your colors, the more you understand your shape, the easier it will be to determine where you fit in and where you don't—and the clearer it will be who matches your life and who doesn't. Instead of trying to jam the puzzle piece into any available opening, you'll have clearer discernment of what and who fit into your calling and what and who simply don't. If you're struggling to "know yourself" at this point in your life, I highly recommend you consider a season of counseling. Working with someone one-on-one is a life-changing experience that can help you discover the best of who God made you to be.

Clearly Define What and Whom God Has Called You To: Once you know yourself and have a clearer picture of who and what matches your calling, stay focused on that image. There are so many good things in life that it's easy to allow the good to take place of the best. For example, I have so many incredible ministry invitations and opportunities that come my way in any given year. But realistically, I can't do them all. My time doesn't stretch that far, because just like you, I only have 24 hours in a day, 7 days in a week, and 365 days in a year. This means I've had to get really good at recognizing what God has called me to, and saying no to everything that doesn't align with those priorities. I've had to set a clearly defined boundary around the things that matter most to me, and clarify what order I'm choosing to prioritize them.

My relationship with God, which includes the health of my soul, comes first. My husband comes second, and making sure to invest in the number-one ministry God has called me to, which is my marriage. My family comes next, because I strongly believe I can't pour out to others if I'm not pouring into the lives of my children first. Once I know those things are in order, I make room for the ministry opportunities that come my way, always considering how my decisions will impact my top three priorities. Even though ministering, serving God, and helping people heal is the passion of my heart, I've had to set many limits around my ministry with regards to how much to do and when. I probably say no to something or someone on a daily basis. And I don't even feel guilty about it. You know why? Because every time I say no to something good, I am ultimately saying yes to something great. I'm saying no to what others call me to, and yes to what God calls me to. Once you've clearly outlined your unique essentials, you won't get distracted by peripheral things.

Own Only What's Yours: Something else that helps me set boundaries is remembering that I am only responsible for my portion. I am only in charge of the things God has asked me to take ownership of. I am not responsible for the expectations, obligations, demands, desires, and wishes of others. I am not responsible for the emotions, actions, thoughts, behaviors, and reactions of others either. I don't define my calling by external pressure, but by internal prayer. I don't define my calling based on what people want me to do and then consult with God; I consult with God first and then make decisions based on what's He's asked of me.

> I don't define my calling by external pressure, but by internal prayer.

The other mindset shift that has really helped me with setting boundaries is having a proper perspective of who I am and my limits. These days, I refuse to believe the lie that I am "the only one" who can do something. If I truly believe I am the only one who can counsel this person, or the only one who can help this church, or the only one who can speak at this event, then I will certainly lose my focus and get bogged down by others' demands. So I've had to shift my perspective and acknowledge that I am not the only one. I am not indispensable. God has raised up an army of other people who are also tasked with fulfilling His calling. I can only do what I am called to do. God will be the One to fill in the gaps. This mindset shift frees me up to own what's mine alone, and I have to trust God with everything and everyone else that belongs to Him. It's a lot easier to set limits when you truly believe God will take care of the things, people, and obligations you can't. You can only own what's yours to own.

> You can only own what's yours to own.

Get Comfortable Saying No and Not Now: Please understand that saying no isn't anti-Christian. Saying no is simply an acknowledgement of your capacity and your human limitations. In fact, I believe it takes utmost humility to be able to say no. Christians often falsely believe that Jesus said yes to everything and everyone, when in reality, He set many boundaries and limits throughout His time here. In fact, He often used the phrase "My time has not yet come" to remind His followers that He wasn't on their timeline but on God's (John 7:6 ESV). Contrary to popular belief, Jesus wasn't a yes-man. In Mark 1, the disciples were looking for Jesus because He was in high demand. But before the sun came up, He had gone off to pray in solitude. When they finally found Jesus, they said, "Everyone is looking for you!" (verse 37). Jesus knew everyone was looking for Him, yet He still wanted to be alone to pray. It takes wisdom and discernment to protect the calling God has on your life, especially when the expectations of others are looming.

Then, when the disciples asked Jesus to return to Capernaum where He had been performing miracles, He told them it was time to go to the next town instead (Mark 1:35-38). He had a clear vision of what God wanted Him to do, and He didn't get sidetracked. Even when it meant He had to say no and not now. To learn to protect what matters, you must get used to saying no and not now.

DON'T GET DISTRACTED

When your heart is aligned with God's calling on your life, setting boundaries and limits becomes a tool for staying focused! You get comfortable making hard decisions and not getting distracted because your eyes are fixed on the finish line. I like how the New Living Translation puts it in Proverbs 4:25-27: "Look straight ahead, and fix your eyes on what lies before you. Mark out a straight path for your feet; stay on the safe path. Don't get sidetracked; keep your feet from following evil." Don't get sidetracked—don't get distracted! Keep your eyes on the goal, which is your sacred calling. In order to protect what matters, you have to remember that God's plans for your life are more important than any expectation, obligation, or demand the world may try to place on you. You have to believe that God > Man, and then live that way.

Verse for Reflection

It is dangerous to be concerned with what others think of you, but if you trust the LORD, you are safe (Proverbs 29:25 GNT).

Today's Rhythm: PROTECT YOUR CALLING

1. When it comes to your own people-pleasing tendencies, on a scale of zero to ten (zero being unfazed, ten being extremely influenced), how influenced are you by the demands and expectations of others? Why or why not?

2. Do you consider yourself a yes-person or a no-person? How do you currently choose what you say yes to, and what you say no to?

3. Have you been able to identify the people and purposes God has called you to in this season of your life? Take some time to list what you would consider the essentials and priorities in your life.

4. What are some boundaries and limitations you have set (or will begin to set) around your life to protect what God has called you to in your personal and spiritual life? With your friends and family? With your ministry and career?

SAVOR

Caring for Your Soul by Being Present,
Practicing Gratitude, and
Intentionally Enjoying Life

Chapter 15

ENJOY LIFE

For the Fun of It

I'LL NEVER FORGET THE YEAR WHEN GOD TOLD ME TO have more fun. I was going through an incredibly demanding time in both my personal life and my professional life. In response, I was actively seeking God and asking Him how He wanted me to best navigate this difficult season. I'm a passionate person by nature, and when I do something, I want to do it well. So I was looking to Jesus to help me figure out my next steps. To guide me toward a plan of action. To help me respond to my calling to the best of my ability. And one day, amid my persistent prayers, I felt Him smiling down on me and saying, "I just want you to have more fun."

Huh? What was that, God? There are souls at stake, people in need of healing, injustices in need of confrontation! I have an entire to-do list here. Fun? That can't be accurate. I don't think I heard You correctly. Would You mind repeating that so I can write it down this time?

And there it was again, like an unexpected ray of sunshine on a cloudy day: "I want you to have more fun."

Have you ever had one of those moments when you felt God speaking directly to your heart? This was such a moment for me. Except I really hadn't expected that answer. In fact, His words didn't really answer the series of questions I had on my list to begin with! Here I was, trying to figure out what my next steps should be, but God wanted me to enjoy the journey instead of obsessing over it—which is easier said than done for type A people like myself. I like to have a plan, a checklist, and a timeline. I even present my prayer requests in checklist form! I want to get things done in the most efficient way possible. I don't want to waste time smelling the roses or dancing in the rain when I've got a mission to accomplish. Or at least, I used to be that way.

JOY IS A GIFT

A lot has changed for me since that year when God told me to have more fun. Not only was it a life-changing perspective shift for me, but I've also seen the incredible value of enjoying the journey of life rather than just getting through it. For some people, fun and enjoyment comes easy. For others like me, enjoying life and having fun is a discipline that must be practiced. It's a mindset that must be unearthed. It's a rhythm that should be prioritized for the health of my soul.

Scripture talks a lot about enjoying life! Maybe I didn't see it before because I wasn't looking for it. I could certainly tell you all the verses about *living* for Jesus, *doing* for Jesus, and *dying* for Jesus—but *enjoying* Jesus?

> Enjoying life becomes a catalyst for doing the work that God has called us to do!

Enjoying life? Having fun? That wasn't really on my radar as a spiritual rhythm. In Ecclesiastes 8:15, Solomon says it like this: "I decided it was more important to enjoy life because the best thing people can do in this life is to eat, drink, and enjoy life. At least that will help people enjoy the hard work God gave them to do during their life on earth" (ERV). When we consider it this way, enjoying life becomes a catalyst for doing the work God has called us to do! It provides the right balance we need to keep moving forward. Proverbs 17:22 reminds us that "a joyful heart is good medicine" (ESV). With all the burdens, responsibilities, and hardships in our world, I wonder if we've lost the wonder of a joyful heart.

Jesus was filled with joy (Luke 10:21). In fact, it seems joy isn't just optional; it's evidence of the Holy Spirit! The joy of the Holy Spirit is a common phrase in God's Word (1 Thessalonians 1:6-7). Not only was Jesus marked by the joy of the Spirit of God, but He wants that same joy to be in us as well (John 15:11). I truly believe that by God's Spirit and power, we can find joy no matter our circumstances (Philippians 4:11-12). But what I've also realized is that it's also up to us to find joy—to seek it out! We need to be deliberate in our joy and in the act of enjoying and rejoicing (Psalm 32:11; Philippians 4:4). We need to live so that joy follows us wherever we go, because we are connected to the source of all joy. This has really challenged my perspective and my life. I want to be known for my joy. Not my efficiency, not my accomplishments, not my to-do list—but

> We need to live so that joy follows us wherever we go, because we are connected to the source of all joy.

my joy. The same joy that lived inside the heart of Jesus lives in me today, and the joy of the Lord is my strength (Nehemiah 8:10). Joy is a gift—one I must acknowledge, receive, and pursue in my daily life.

CONTAGIOUS JOY

Have you ever been around someone who just radiated so much joy, it made you want to be near them? Right now, that person for me is our son Ethan. He's our little unexpected gift. After a traumatic miscarriage, we weren't planning on having any more children. But then God gifted us with a surprise pregnancy, and our rainbow baby was born! He is literally the cutest child on the face of planet earth. He's three years old right now, and if you follow me on Instagram, you know the cuteness I'm talking about! He's full of joy, with a smile plastered on his sweet face from the moment he wakes up to the moment he goes to bed. He discovers things to love every day, from new foods to new activities, to new games to new words, and he always says with utter and complete enthusiasm, "I wuv [love] this so much!" Just being around him makes the happiness factor in the room increase tenfold. His joy overflows onto everyone around him. Everyone feels it. Everyone notices it. Everyone says the same thing: that joy follows him wherever he goes. And I pray it does for the rest of his days.

I wonder if that's what it felt like to be around Jesus, amid an atmosphere of deep joy. Jesus radiated joy from the inside out, in a way that overflowed onto everyone He interacted with and everything He did. Not only did He exude joy, but He also enjoyed life! When I think about Jesus enjoying life, my mind goes to the story of the wedding in Cana. Like I've mentioned before, I come from a Middle Eastern background. And Middle Eastern people know how to have a good time—especially at weddings! It's an all-day, sometimes multiday, experience of food, fun, and festivities. There's dancing and singing and eating and laughing and celebrating.

Have you ever thought about why Jesus was on the guest list of this type of wedding? John 2:2 tells us that "Jesus and his disciples had also been invited to the wedding." And not only was He invited, but He showed up! And not only did He show up, but He kept the wedding festivities going by turning water into wine—the best wine, as a matter of fact (John 2:7-10). Jesus showed up, and when He did, He brought the joy with Him. I love how Max Lucado puts it in his book *He Gets Us*:

> May I state an opinion that could raise an eyebrow? May I tell you why I think Jesus went to that wedding in Cana? I think he went to the wedding to—now hold on, hear me out —I think Jesus went to the wedding to have fun.
>
> Think about it. It had been a tough season. This wedding occurred after he had just spent forty days in the desert. No food or water. A standoff with the devil...A job change. He had left home. It hadn't been easy. A break would be

welcome. A good meal with some good wine and some good friends...Well, it sounded pretty nice.

So off they went.

His purpose wasn't to turn the water into wine. That was a favor for his friends.

His purpose wasn't to show his power. The wedding host didn't even know what Jesus did.

His purpose wasn't to preach. There is no record of a sermon.

This leaves only one reason. Fun...

Jesus was a likable fellow. And his disciples should be the same. I'm not talking debauchery, drunkenness, and adultery. I'm not endorsing compromise, coarseness, or obscenity. I am simply crusading for the freedom to enjoy a good joke, enliven a dull party, and appreciate a fun evening.

Maybe these thoughts catch you by surprise. They do me. It's been a while since I pegged Jesus as a party lover. But he was. His foes accused him of eating too much, drinking too much, and hanging out with the wrong people! I must confess: it's been a while since I've been accused of having too much fun. How about you?[1]

FOR THE JOY OF IT

I love that picture of Jesus, attending a wedding simply for the fun of it. And I wonder if your soul could use a little more fun in this season of life. I wonder if maybe you've lost the joy you once had. Or maybe you've been so bogged down by the burdens of life, for as long as you can remember, that you never got into the habit of creating rhythms of joy—of doing something just for the delight of it.

Think about the things that bring you joy. What are they? Do you have any hobbies or interests, activities or experiences that make you smile at the thought of them? Ever since God spoke to my heart about having more fun, I've taken seriously the task of investing in the things that bring me joy and then connecting with God through those things! It's a gift to enjoy this life. Some things that bring me joy are taking a walk in nature, exploring a new city or town, drinking a good cup of coffee with a friend, feeling my feet in the sand by the ocean, jumping on the trampoline with my kids, floating in the pool with a good audiobook in my ear, cooking a new recipe for dinner, sitting on my deck during sunset with good company, trying a new restaurant with my husband, going on an impromptu road trip, and so much more. I've learned to both find the joy and create the joy in the time God has given me. And not only that, I've learned the importance of making it a priority—allowing enjoyment to lighten the burden that inevitably comes amid the work of this life.

My friends, this life is a gift, with everything in it. What if we were to enjoy it? To *really* enjoy it? To have more celebrations, more laughs, more smiles, more peace, and more contentment than ever before. To practice rhythms of fun…for nothing other than the joy of it.

Verse for Reflection

I decided it was more important to enjoy life because the best thing people can do in this life is to eat, drink, and enjoy life. At least that will help people enjoy the hard work God gave them to do during their life on earth (Ecclesiastes 8:15 ERV).

Today's Rhythm: FOR THE FUN OF IT

1. What thoughts and feelings come up for you when you think about the idea of Jesus enjoying life and bringing joy? What type of atmosphere do you bring when you walk into a room?

2. In the past six months, has your life been marked more by joy or by stress? Why or why not? What has been robbing you of your joy?

3. Make a list of ten life-giving activities that bring you joy and fill you up in healthy ways. (It might be hard for some of you to think of ten!)

4. What are some practical ways you can you make space for those activities in this season of life?

Chapter 16

SAVOR LIFE

Learn to Be Present

WHEN YOU THINK OF THE WORD SAVOR, WHAT COMES to mind?

I instantly think of dark chocolate.

I imagine putting a piece of dark chocolate in my mouth, balancing it on the center of my tongue, and letting the rich, melty goodness slowly overwhelm my taste buds. Even as I think about it, my mouth is puckering up a little from just the thought of that bittersweetness. I love dark chocolate. I love it so much that I make a point not to scarf it down, even though I could easily and mindlessly grab a piece of dark chocolate while I'm doing the dishes, writing this book, or watching a movie. But I don't. I usually save it for after hours. If you've read my book *Choosing Marriage*, you'll remember the story about the chocolate stash in my nightstand (the one that instigated a huge fight between me and John when he messed with my chocolate stash). Go read about it, laugh, and learn from our marriage mistakes.

It's true that I still have a small stash of really good dark chocolate in the upper drawer of my nightstand. And I'm not talking Hershey's Special Dark Chocolate. (That stuff is mostly sugar anyway.) I'm talking the bittersweet-but-mostly-bitter type of dark chocolate you get at 85 percent or 90 percent cocoa. The type of dark chocolate my three-year-old would spit out because it's a little too bitter. Yep, that's the stuff. I keep it in my nightstand for two reasons: one, because it's a great hiding spot; and two, because it's the kind of dark chocolate I want to savor. I want to enjoy it little by little, enjoying the pieces with no distractions. A bar like that could last me a few months, and I enjoy it the most that way! What's something in your life you savor?

I want to savor my whole life in a similar way—not rushing through it or focusing on simply getting to the end of it. I want to appreciate it, cherish it, and get the most out of it. I want to slow down and savor it moment by moment, memory by memory, and take it all in. And I can tell you, it's much harder to do that with life than it is to do with a piece of dark chocolate.

SENSORY OVERLOAD

It's hard to savor life when so many things are competing for your attention. At any given moment, we're bombarded by sensory overload from our devices buzzing in our pockets, to the lawn mower outside, to our kids playing (or fighting) nearby, to the TV and music in the background, to the UPS delivery person at the door, to the baby calling for our attention, to the hundreds of thoughts swirling around in our minds. So much noise, internal and external. Distractions everywhere.

Add to that how we're often moving on autopilot, mindlessly getting through the day rather than being present in it. Have you ever driven to work, to church, or to an errand and found yourself at your destination without remembering how you actually got there? Maybe your mind was consumed by a stressful situation, and you were ruminating on that while your body drove you to your destination. Autopilot mode. We're so in our heads sometimes that we don't tune in to what's happening around us, to the life we're supposed to be living right here and right now. How can you savor something you're not even aware of? How can you make the most of something you're not even paying attention to?

RIGHT HERE, RIGHT NOW

Jesus understood the importance of savoring life. He understood the value of being present and aware of what was going on in the moment. He understood the many distractions that could easily prevent us from savoring the gift of life.

When I read the Gospels through the lens of soul care, so many little practices of how Jesus lived His life stand out to me. Matthew 13:1 is one such verse: "Jesus went out of the house and sat by the lake." Jesus sat by the lake. Why I never really saw that verse before, I couldn't say—but it was so affirming and meaningful to read. I don't know about you, but I absolutely love water. I find bodies of water to be so relaxing. I love sitting by the ocean, a lake, a canal, or a river. Just give me a pond, and I'll be happy! I love sitting, looking out at the water, taking in the moment. I delight in the scent of the water, the feel of the cool wind on my face, and the sounds of the birds, waves, and water splashing against the rocks. I could sit there for hours without anything to do, read, or accomplish. In those moments, I am truly savoring this gift of life. And then I think about Jesus…just sitting by the lake. I imagine Him deeply breathing in the fresh air and whispering a prayer to the Father. I imagine Him in that moment, in all of His humanity, simply savoring life.

I imagine that Jesus made the most of these opportunities—to pace Himself and look around with a smile at this gift, these people, this world. But because He was in such high demand, a large crowd soon gathered around Him—right there in His happy place by the lake. And soon enough He started telling stories, as He loved to do. He told them the parable of the sower. In this parable, a man sowed seeds—but each time he did, obstacles prevented the seeds from taking root. One of those obstacles is the obstacle of distraction (Matthew 13:22). The worries, distractions, and hustle of life were like the thorns that choked the good seeds and prevented them from thriving. And I wonder, if right there on the lake, Jesus was inviting the crowds to stop and consider the distractions they faced each day. Distractions that were keeping them from fully embracing God's truth. Distractions that were preventing them from being present—right then and there, to the Son of God and what He was offering them in that moment: Himself.

When I think of savoring life, I think of Jesus spending time with His friends Mary and Martha. You know the story. Jesus went to pay a visit to His friends in the town of Bethany. He was there to spend time with them, to be present with them. To savor the gifts of friendship and community. But Martha had so much to do—she was hosting this dinner party! She had food to prepare, a house to clean, people to serve. There's always a to-do list, isn't there? There's always something to do that ends up preventing us from simply *being*. Because you can't be and do all at the same time.

Meanwhile, as "Martha was distracted by all the preparations that had to be made," Mary was sitting by the feet of Jesus, savoring every word that came from His mouth, joyfully taking in His very presence. And Jesus looked lovingly at Martha, who was probably feeling burned-out and unappreciated, and said, "Martha, Martha…you are worried and upset about many things, but few things are needed—or indeed only one. Mary has chosen what is better, and it will not be taken away from her" (Luke 10:40-42). The one thing that couldn't be taken away from Mary was the gift of the moment, the presence of Jesus. She was savoring their friendship with everything inside of her. Absolutely nothing else was more important than taking it all in. And she did.

Hear me on this, my friends: Sometimes the healthiest way to live is not the most efficient way to live. I have to speak those words over the Martha that lives inside of me—the side of me that loves my to-do lists, getting things done in a timely fashion, doing as much as I can in as little time as possible, accomplishing and completing and moving on to the next thing. It's easy for me to quickly answer that one last text, check off that final thing on the to-do list, or write that one last email. I am a doer by nature. And I speak the language of efficiency. But efficiency is often the enemy of savoring life. Because the goal of the former is to get through it, while the goal of the latter is to make the most of it. You simply cannot rush and savor all at the same time. Jesus was calling Martha to stop and savor. He was inviting her into the richness of the moment, right then and right there.

I wonder if the same goes for me and for you. Might God be inviting us into the richness of this moment, right here and right now? What is happening in this season of your life that you are invited to savor? What is God doing in the world around you? What is taking place right before your eyes, and are you seeing it? Are you experiencing it? Are you even aware of it? Or are you distracted by the many plans, checklists, and to-dos? Are your phones and other devices robbing you of the one thing that is needed? Are you constantly looking down when you could be looking up?

> Sometimes the healthiest way to live is not the most efficient way to live.

When was the last time you, like Jesus, just stopped to sit by the lake? How often do you stop to look around at what is happening around you, and simply soak it all in?

THE OPPOSITE OF MINDLESS

How often are you mindlessly living life, just getting from here to there, finding yourself at the end of a long day that you hardly remember? We're all guilty of it. But the opposite of mindlessness is *mindfulness*. When we're mindful, we're focused. We're acutely aware. We're purposefully blocking out the distractions and looking around. In counseling we often refer to mindfulness as a powerful practice that helps us stop and become more aware of what's going on inside of you and around you. It means an opportunity to slow down and savor life. One mindfulness activity you might learn if you work with me or one of the counselors on my team[1] is a noticing activity. In this activity, you practice becoming aware of what's going on around you by tuning in to your five senses. Let's stop for a moment and do this mindfulness activity together.

FIVE-MINUTE MINDFULNESS SENSORY ACTIVITY

Sight

Become aware of something you see around you right now. Look at it and notice its unique details. Be grateful for it. Take a moment to thank God for your sight. Then ask Him to help you honor Him with the things you see and to open the eyes of your heart to see Him more clearly (Matthew 6:22; Ephesians 1:18).

Sound

Become aware of something you hear around you right now. Notice the sound. Be grateful for it. Take a moment to thank God for your hearing. Then ask Him to open your ears, so you may tune in to the spiritual truths He wants you to have the ears to hear (Matthew 11:15).

Taste

Become aware of something you taste right now. It could be something you're eating, like dark chocolate or a piece of gum or a mint, or even just the taste of your mouth. Notice the sensation. Be grateful for it. Take a moment to thank God for your taste. Then ask Him to help you honor Him with the things you eat and enjoy—and more so, to taste and know that He is good (Psalm 34:8).

Smell

Become aware of something you smell around you right now. Notice the unique scent. Be grateful for it. Take a moment to thank God for your sense of smell. Then ask Him to help your life become an aroma that's pleasing to Him (2 Corinthians 2:15).

Touch

Become aware of something you feel around you right now. It could be the sensation of your clothing, the chair you're sitting on, the ground under your feet, or even the breeze around you. Notice the unique feeling. Be grateful for it. Take a moment to thank God for your touch, and ask Him to help you honor Him with all your senses wherever your feet may go (Isaiah 52:7).

To savor life, you must be acutely aware of it. You must open your eyes to what's happening around you, and slow down enough to delight in it. This mindfulness practice is something you can do anytime, anywhere. In fact, I often stop throughout my day and take a mental pause in order to soak in what's happening around me and the people God has placed near me right here and right now: the sight of my kids playing in the yard at the glow of sunset; the scent of the neighbors' firepit reminding me of the people God has placed right next door; the feeling of my husband's hand interlocked with mine as we sit on our back porch; the taste and feel of ice water as it hits my mouth; the sounds of kids laughing and the birds chirping. And when I do stop to delight in them, I smile as I feel Jesus closer than ever before—sitting next to me, reminding me to savor this life. May we all become more aware of His presence and learn to be present, right here and right now.

> To savor life, you must be acutely aware of it.

Verse for Reflection

You are worried and distracted by many things;
but only one thing is necessary (Luke 10:41-42 NASB).

Today's Rhythm: LEARN TO BE PRESENT

1. Do you tend to rush through things or live on autopilot? Why or why not?

2. List the internal or external distractions that tend to keep you from savoring life.

3. Take a break to practice the five-minute mindfulness sensory activity from this chapter. Afterward, write down what you observed.

4. Consider this question today: What is God doing right here and right now in your life? What is something you can savor or someone you can be fully present with today?

Chapter 17

CELEBRATE LIFE

Thanksgiving and Praise

I'VE BEEN READING THE BOOK OF LEVITICUS LATELY. I know, I know, talk about a real hook to draw you into this chapter. I suggest not using that line if you're ever on a first date, because there are probably better conversation starters out there than the book of Leviticus. But hear me out.

If you don't know, the book of Leviticus is essentially a book of rules and regulations for the Israelites. It's like the instruction manual God gave His people to keep them spiritually and physically healthy. It also provides guidelines for how they were to present their sacrificial offerings to the Lord. Needless to say, most people wouldn't consider Leviticus a page-turner.

But as I immersed myself in the book of Leviticus, something that really struck me was the concept of the thanksgiving offering. This offering is also referred to as the peace or fellowship offering. It was a sacrifice given for the pure and unadulterated reason of gratitude—to celebrate and thank God for who He was and what He had done. Of all the sacrifices outlined in the

Levitical law, this offering was the only one that was not *required*. It was optional. You didn't have to do it, but you were welcomed into it. It was to be a freewill offering. This offering was often made for one of three reasons:

1. To thank God for an unexpected blessing.
2. To acknowledge the fulfillment of a vow or an answered prayer.
3. To make a public gesture of general gratitude to God.

In essence, it was a way to celebrate all that God had done!

Another thing that set this offering apart was how it was shared with the worshippers. According to theologian Warren Wiersbe, "After the priest had completed the sacrifice, a large portion of the meat went to him; the rest went to the offerer, who could then enjoy a feast with his family and friends. Since the Jews didn't often slaughter their precious animals for meat, a dinner of beef or lamb would be a special occasion."[1] The thanksgiving offering wasn't just for God; it was also for the worshippers too.

I was so touched by reading about the thanksgiving offering and the idea that this thanksgiving celebration is also for me. I am the one who benefits from the celebration! I am invited to come freely, without obligation or requirement, to thank God because I am in relationship with Him! Gratitude naturally creates connection because it allows me to draw near to God. And He is always available to me! The invitation to gratitude and connection is there for those who embrace it. I had to stop and ask myself: *In what ways do I commemorate, celebrate, or give thanks to God for the things He's done for me? How often do I make it a point to stop throughout my day and turn my attention toward God in gratitude and thanksgiving?* Not only is expressing gratitude an opportunity to give God the glory for all He has done, but also it benefits me because gratitude moves my heart into healthy places.

GRATITUDE IS FOR YOU

The science on the benefits of practicing gratitude is overwhelming. Study after study tells us that the practice of gratitude is directly correlated to our overall well-being.[2] Gratitude also impacts how we perceive stress, and ultimately, the state of our mental health.[3] It changes our perspective on life and enhances our mental well-being.[4] It naturally decreases our stress chemical (cortisol) and helps us to balance our mood. Essentially, we are happier, healthier, less stressed, and further from burnout when we have a routine of gratitude in our lives. This is why many counselors and psychologists recommend the practice of gratitude journaling as part of your counseling process. It's an invitation to direct your thinking and focus on the good when it's much easier by default to focus on everything that's not good in life.

> The thanksgiving offering was the only offering to be shared with both God and the worshipper.

I believe it's so beautiful and symbolic that the thanksgiving offering was the only offering to be shared with both God and the worshipper. It's as though God knew this practice was just as beneficial for us, and by inviting us into the practice of thanksgiving, He was also inviting us into emotional and mental well-being.

Jesus Himself modeled rhythms of thanksgiving on a regular basis. He lived in a constant state of thankfulness, and He encouraged us to do the same. He practiced gratitude—both in anticipation of the good times and in the aftermath of the hard times. He looked up to heaven and gave thanks to God before feeding the 5,000 (Matthew 14:19), but He also looked up to heaven with a grateful heart after the death of His friend Lazarus (John 11:41-42). He thanked God for truth, and specifically for revealing His truth to those who were willing to receive it (Luke 10:21). And He often thanked God out loud to demonstrate gratitude for us. Because gratitude ushers us into the presence of God (Psalm 100:4). It opens the eyes of our hearts to see God and what He is doing more vividly, all while dimming our tendency to fixate on the negative things around us.

Scripture is packed with passages about the importance of thanksgiving because living with gratitude matters both scientifically and spiritually

(Colossians 4:2; 1 Thessalonians 5:18; Philippians 4:6; 1 Timothy 4:4-5; Psalm 69:30; 92:1-2; 106:1; Hebrews 12:28-29). Truly, the person who benefits most from a life of gratitude is you.

GRATITUDE JOURNALING

If you struggle to feel gratitude in your life, I encourage you to start with a simple gratitude journal. Get a blank notebook, or maybe the one you use for your Bible reading or quiet time. Dedicate one page, or five minutes at some part of your day, to writing out at least five things you are grateful for. Try and list five different things each day for the first seven days, ending the week with 35 unique things. Be as specific as possible. For example, instead of just writing "my family," write something like, "I'm grateful for the time I was able to spend with my family yesterday at dinner and for the many laughs we have together." Consider being grateful for things that didn't happen or didn't go according to plan, as well as for things that went well. True story: Just this morning, when I sat down to write this chapter, I realized that a technological error prevented this book's working document from syncing to the drive where it's autosaved. It hadn't been syncing for over three weeks, and I didn't realize it until I tried to open the document today and it opened to an outdated version from six chapters ago. I was devastated. I had lost almost a third of my manuscript! Needless to say, I shed some tears when I finally understood it was likely gone forever. But, thank Jesus, my brilliant husband—after digging around for some time— was able to manually restore the most recent version from somewhere in the deepest, darkest parts of my computer. Without his help, the draft would have been swallowed up forever. Talk about thanksgiving! I may need to offer a literal sacrifice tonight. Kids, we're having lamb for dinner!

But honestly, how often do we spend time with a heart of gratitude for the things we were spared? Thank You, God, for the document that wasn't deleted! For the sickness that was avoided! For the car accident that didn't happen! For the relationships that didn't work out! For all the things we don't even know we were spared from, but here we are today! There is so much to be grateful for, if we'll only open our eyes to see it and then open our mouths to acknowledge it. (I'll also give you a few more guidelines for gratitude journaling in the Today's Rhythm portion at the end of the chapter.)

> There is so much to be grateful for, if we'll only open our eyes to see it and then open our mouths to acknowledge it.

PRAISE AND THANKSGIVING

If thanksgiving is focusing our hearts and minds on what God has done, praise is focusing our hearts and minds on who God is. It's our opportunity to celebrate His character, His attributes, His qualities, His goodness, His faithfulness, His holiness, His splendor. And thanksgiving and praise go hand in hand! Psalm 7:17 proclaims, "I will give thanks to the LORD because of his righteousness; I will sing the praises of the name of the LORD Most High." Not only that, but praise and thanksgiving often come with singing—as though you just can't help but let it out when you're filled with the gratitude of who He is and what He's done! Psalm 95:2 says, "Let us come before him with thanksgiving and extol him with music and song." Even Jesus sang songs of worship! I bet you never caught that verse in the Bible, did you? But now that you're looking for it, you'll find it in Matthew 26:30: "When they had sung a hymn, they went out to the Mount of Olives." Something about imagining Jesus singing songs to heaven makes the act of worship all the more meaningful!

The experience of worship resonates with me, to the point of it being one of my favorite things! There's nothing that can bring heaven down to earth, change the atmosphere of my day, and shift the attitude of my spirit the way worship can. I love to put on some worship music and enter a mindset of praise. All of a sudden, I am no longer looking around at all the things going on around me, but instead am now looking up at the God who goes before me and behind me. The great and glorious God who lives inside of me. He is worthy of my praise, my honor, and my thanksgiving! Incorporating a time of praise and worship into my daily routine has been a really important addition to my personal life and my practice of soul care. Filling my ears, my mouth, and my heart with songs of praise and worship has become an integral part of my life, whether in the car, in the kitchen while loading the dishwasher, with the kids at the start of the day, amid my workday, or outside while sitting on the deck.

Here are some of the more unique places I've been known to have worship songs playing: while riding my bike (I have a phone holder on the handlebars so I can blast music while I'm biking); while on a walk with my kids (the toddler's stroller has a cupholder that acts as a fabulous amplification system for my phone—you should try it!); and even in the bathroom (thank God for waterproof speakers). Whatever I'm doing and whenever I'm doing it, I want my mind to be set on praise—because God is worthy of that and so much more. And not only is He worthy of praise, but the gratitude also radically impacts my heart! I reap the benefits of a praise-filled heart when my emotions become stabilized, my perspective shifts, my mind finds peace, and my soul becomes less burdened by the troubles and cares of this world.

I know this isn't just true for me. I have worked with countless clients who have remarkably shifted their mental and emotional well-being by practicing gratitude and praise. Just by incorporating daily rhythms of thanksgiving, their mindsets began to transform. I think of Dustin, who struggled so much with a negative mindset when we met in our first counseling session. According to him, everything in his life had been so difficult, and he was filled with regrets. Career struggles, relationship failures, and interpersonal problems had him feeling perpetually frustrated and discouraged. With time, I helped Dustin get to the roots of some of his negative thinking patterns, and then begin incorporating rhythms of gratitude into his life to replace those old and unhealthy patterns. It changed everything for him. Just last week, I told him how proud I was of him for how far he'd come in his mindset. He's no longer the negative guy I met in our first session; he's now defined by hope, a balanced perspective, and the ability to see the good in the life he's been given. Honestly, he's also much more pleasant to be around. His gratitude radiates from his life! Like I said before, thanksgiving is also for you. It's for your benefit. It's for your peace of mind. It's for your perspective shift. It changes you from the inside out. And I would even go so far as to say that gratitude is a prerequisite to a healthy soul. So take some time today to celebrate life. Take some time for thanksgiving and praise.

Verse for Reflection

*I will give thanks to the LORD with my whole heart;
I will recount all of your wonderful deeds (Psalm 9:1 ESV).*

Today's Rhythm: THANKSGIVING AND PRAISE

1. How can you incorporate a rhythm of thanksgiving and worship into your daily routine?

2. Consider five things you are grateful for today and write about them.

3. Consider five things you appreciate and adore about God and write about them. Spend some time praising Him for who He is.

4. Commit to a week of gratitude journaling. Here are some tips to help you get started:
   - Grab a journal and pen or pencil. You can also choose to type on a computer or a phone document.

   - Take at least five minutes at some point during your day (ideally the start of your day) to think about five things you're grateful for. Then write down your chosen things. Be as specific as you can during this time. Try not to list simple two-word answers such as "my family," but explain exactly what you are grateful for about your family.

   - Think creatively and consider writing about the things that didn't happen that you are grateful for. For example: "I'm grateful we got safely to our destination without an accident."

- Continue this practice for seven days to get you started. Consider increasing the amount of time you spend on gratitude journaling. Then contemplate incorporating it into your routine a few times a week.

TUNE IN

Caring for Your Soul by Having Insight
and Understanding of Your Inner World

Chapter 18

A PERSON OF INSIGHT

Tune In

THE BRAVEST JOURNEY YOU WILL EVER TAKE IS THE journey toward looking inside your soul. I'm convinced this is why so many people avoid it. Some people will do anything and everything to distract themselves from looking in. They'll plan their next fun activity, research their dream vacations, and immerse themselves in all kinds of distractions so they can continue to look ahead and not have to look inward. On the other hand, others aren't necessarily avoiding it, but they're completely unaware of their internal world. They've never been taught about the value of looking inside or even how to do it, so they spend most of their time just looking around. They are much more in tune to the world that's going on around them than they are to the world inside of them. They notice people, places, and things but aren't as in tune with their emotions, thoughts, and behaviors. They can give you all the information, statistics, and data you asked for (or didn't ask for), but they seem to come up short when you ask them how they're *feeling*. But whether they're avoidant or just unaware, both types of people have one thing in common: the absence of insight.

I earnestly believe that the most important ingredient to a healthy soul is the ability to look in—to have insight and understanding about what's going on inside of you. To go into the deepest places of your heart, and then come back up with awareness and understanding. I guess you could say this is the essential the work we help people do in counseling.

If I had to choose a single passage of Scripture to describe the work I get to help people do as a counselor, it would most certainly be Proverbs 20:5, which says: "The purposes of a person's heart are deep waters, but one who has insight draws them out." Our souls are like deep waters! The purposes of our heart—our underlying motivations, the reasons we do what we do—are literally at the depths of who we are. So deep down, in fact, many people aren't even aware of them. But according to this passage, a person who has insight *draws them out*. Do you see what an active process that is? To draw the water from the depths of who you are is not something that happens passively. You've got to be proactive about it.

It's worth mentioning that the idea of drawing water, specifically in ancient times, wasn't an easy process. It was nothing like turning on the high-class modern-day faucets and enjoying the stream of cold water. At our house, you don't even have to touch anything for the faucet to turn on. You just put your hands close enough, and the sensors turn on the stream of water for you! But when this passage was written, the concept of drawing water had much more significance. It was an active, deliberate, and intentional process. Because of the desert heat, you often had to plan your trip to the well at dusk or dawn. It usually required a long walk with empty buckets in each hand. Once you reached the well, you'd have to put down your bucket and draw it back up filled with heavy water. This process of drawing water required energy, effort, intentionality, and strength. It demanded perseverance, patience, and commitment.[1]

GOING DEEP

And so it goes for us. A person of insight commits to drawing from the deep waters of their life. The process requires intentionally going down to the depths and discovering the underlying motivations, thoughts, beliefs, and feelings that make us who we are. In counseling, I often refer to this as "getting to the roots." I call it getting to the roots because an issue is not dealt with if you only address its surface. For example, take the weeds in your garden. One way to remove them is by snipping off the portion that's above ground. But while this tactic may work for a few days, if you're not pulling it from the root, the weed will be back again in no time. The underlying things are what ultimately influence what we do and how we behave. In my book *Reset*, I talk a lot about how the process of transformation has to start from the inside out. So often in our lives, we see something we want to change or adjust or fix, and we begin the process by tweaking a few external factors. We want to lose weight, so we sign up for a gym membership. We want to deal with our anger issues, so we take deep breaths and count to ten. We want to spend less money, so we create a budget. All of these steps are helpful and good, but if we're not getting to the bottom of why we do what we do and then addressing and adjusting our motivations, we'll keep repeating patterns again, and again, and again.

> A person of insight commits to drawing from the deep waters of their life.

THOUGHTS → FEELINGS → BEHAVIORS

It's human nature to want to change and adjust things about ourselves. In fact, I would be concerned if you couldn't find something you wanted to change. Transformation and growth are significant parts of the healing process. They're signs of being a person with a healthy soul. Healthy people know a routine assessment needs to take place, so they identify behaviors that are unhealthy and no longer serving them well and replace them with behaviors that are functional and life-giving. But the only way they can do this is by being aware of what's going on deep down in their lives, by being people of *in*sight: people who have a vision for what's happening *inside* of themselves.

If I had to condense the idea of insight into one formula, it would be this: Thoughts → Feelings → Behaviors. Thoughts lead to feelings, which lead to behaviors. Your underlying thoughts and beliefs—also called core beliefs in counseling—have a significant impact on what you feel and experience in life. The first step to insight is becoming aware of some of those underlying narratives—the stories we tell ourselves throughout the day. Where are those stories coming from, and why? What themes or patterns can we identify within the stories happening in our minds?

Often, the stories we tell ourselves have to do with the life experiences we've had. There's a connection to what we believe and what we've been through, especially our experiences from childhood. There's a correlation between our underlying thoughts and the things that have happened to us. Brian was a client I worked with who struggled to believe he wasn't a burden to the people around him. This underlying belief that he was "a burden" led him to thoughts like: *I have to deal with my problems alone because I don't want to burden my wife. She has enough on her plate, and she doesn't need me adding one more thing. If I don't do more, she'll leave me. I can't ask any more of her, so I'll keep my needs to myself.*

You can probably imagine how a stream of underlying thoughts like Brian's caused him to feel isolated and depressed. When I met him and his wife, they were feeling disconnected from one another. Brian was feeling detached, alone, and uncared for. His wife was longing to connect with him but struggling with how withdrawn and emotionally isolated he seemed. These stories he told himself were having a direct impact on his feelings as well as his behavior.

When I asked Brian to look for patterns of feeling detached, alone, and uncared for at other times in his life, specifically in his early development years, he immediately remembered a specific interaction with his father. Growing up in a large family, Brian was number seven out of ten children. He explained that in his large family, it was easy to get overlooked and feel like he was on his own. Brian remembers going to his father one day in need of help, and his exasperated and depleted father responded by saying, "I have nothing left for you, Brian." That phrase stuck with him longer than he ever imagined it would. The words began influencing his core beliefs about himself as well as the world he lived in. Moments like this started shaping his underlying belief system, which affirmed he was a burden, and determined what he thought he could and couldn't expect from the people around him. "Those types of interactions taught me to believe that I was too much, that my needs were too much, and that having needs actually pushed people away rather than brought them close," he said. "I guess I've been unknowingly withdrawing from Linda because, deep down, I don't ever want to feel that feeling of being a burden to her, like I was to my dad." Brian soon began to understand where his underlying beliefs came from, and how those core beliefs were impacting his thoughts, feelings, and behaviors.

> Being a person with a healthy soul means having the insight to see where our thoughts and beliefs have become misaligned, and then realigning our truth to God's Word alone.

TRUTH OVER TRAUMA

Like Brian, it can be really easy for us to believe our trauma over God's truth. We can allow the hard experiences we've been through, rather than the truth of God's unchanging Word, to shape and form our core beliefs. Without our realizing it, the trauma we've been through—the difficult, stressful, and wounding experiences both big and small—begins to shape the beliefs we have about ourselves, God, and others. Trauma becomes the template by which we live our lives. We begin to unintentionally align our beliefs to our traumatic experiences instead of constantly analyzing, assessing, and then adjusting our thoughts and beliefs to the template of God's truth. Being a person with a healthy soul means having the insight to see where our thoughts and beliefs have become misaligned, and then realigning our truth to

God's Word alone. It means living out of the template of truth, rather than the template of trauma.

Jesus consistently used the template of God's truth as the gauge for His internal narrative. There are many examples in Scripture of how He did this, most notably in Matthew 4. The Spirit had led Him to the wilderness for a time of fasting and praying for 40 days and 40 nights in preparation for His time of earthly ministry. At the end of that experience, His body was exhausted and famished. It would be difficult enough being alone in the wilderness for 40 days and 40 nights, much less with nothing to eat! And that's exactly when Satan entered the scene. He saw an opportunity to use a moment of fatigue to try and lace his lies into the story Jesus was telling Himself. With temptation after temptation, lie after lie, Satan tried hard to obscure the truth of God during some of the most vulnerable moments of Jesus's life. But again and again, Jesus held on to the template of God's truth over the template of His trauma. "It is written," Jesus responded (verse 4). Instead of trying to fight back with His own stories, which may have been influenced by His fatigue, hunger, and difficult experiences, He relied on the stories God had already spoken in His Word! After He stood up to Satan's many lies, Satan eventually left (verse 11).

I think about the stories I tell myself in my day-to-day life, and especially in my most vulnerable moments. And I want you to think about them in yours as well. First ask yourself: *When am I most vulnerable to the lies of the enemy?* Is it when you're stressed? Tired? Hungry? Feeling isolated and alone? If you want to be prepared, you have to be aware of the times when you are most vulnerable. Second: *What lies does Satan tell me?* If the enemy could take you down with a lie, what would it be? Does it have something to do with your identity and how you view yourself? Your self-esteem and self-worth? Your competency and relevance? Try and identify the stories you tend to tell yourself that are laced with lies and mistruths.

Third, ask yourself: *Where did this lie come from? When did it begin?* What are the traumas, stressors, and experiences that have led you to entertaining this lie and allowing it to become a part of your life and the stories you tell yourself? And lastly: *How can I begin to trust God's truth over my trauma? How can I fight the lies with the truth of God's Word?* Write out some specific verses that directly talk back to the lies you tend to believe. Then repeat them to yourself every day, like a battle cry. In order for us to find true healing, we need to change the stories we're telling ourselves. We need to replace the template of our trauma with the template of God's truth and allow that to be the one and only narrative that influences everything else.

REWRITING OUR STORIES

I have had the privilege of working with Brian on a regular basis, watching him connect the dots of the untrue stories he's told himself. But I've also watched him begin to rewrite the stories of his life. I've witnessed him shifting his mindset, questioning false beliefs, healing from past wounds, and beginning to trust the truth of God's Word over the truth of his experiences. He's starting to shift what he believes and thinks about himself, God, and others, which is having incredible ripple effects on what he feels, and ultimately how he lives his life. He's working on becoming more vulnerable with himself and with his wife. He's starting to get comfortable with recognizing and sharing his needs, and then trusting the people who love him to meet those needs. He's holding onto the truth that he is not a burden and his needs are not too much, and instead, he's envisioning the smiling face of Jesus, who says to him, "Well done, good and faithful servant" (Matthew 25:23).

It's been beautiful watching him heal, watching him replace his trauma with God's truth. Because no amount of time can heal wounds the way Jesus can when we invite Him into the journey of healing—into some of the deepest places of our hearts. When we invite Him to recenter us and point out the places that are misaligned, we will discover a shift in our thinking. That shift will change the way we feel, and ultimately, what we do. When we rewrite our story using the template of His truth, everything starts to make more sense than ever before.

Maybe you're reading this, and you're already starting to connect the dots. Maybe you can identify the past trauma that has influenced your belief system today. You're starting to come up with a plan for how to face some of those past hurts. You're motivated to start aligning your beliefs with God's truth instead of your past trauma. But maybe you're reading this and you're feeling even more confused, thinking: *How do I even begin to figure out what I'm believing that's harmful and untrue? How do I make sense of what's trauma and what's not? How can I begin healing from some of those painful memories?* I want you to know this is not a process you have to embark on alone. Not only do you have the help of the ultimate Guide and Counselor, the Holy Spirit, but you also have the help of fellow brothers and sisters in Christ who are trained to help you on this journey of self-discovery, insight, and healing. I speak for myself and my entire team of Christian counselors when I say it's our honor and privilege to journey with you into some of the deepest parts of who you are.[2] It's our sincere joy to help you locate the experiences that impacted your core beliefs and examine the trauma-influenced thoughts that need to be realigned to God's truth. You don't have to do this alone. In fact, you're not expected to.

Being a person of insight means we have eyes to see what is going on underneath the surface of our lives. We understand the narratives that are influencing the way we think, feel, and act. We can distinguish unhealthy and faulty thinking from healthy thinking, and then we begin to swap it out for truth.

Verse for Reflection

*The purposes of a person's heart are deep waters,
but one who has insight draws them out (Proverbs 20:5).*

Today's Rhythm: **TUNE IN**

1. Take some time to get alone and go somewhere quiet. Bring a journal and something to write with. Ask yourself: Are you the type of person who avoids their internal world, is simply unaware of their internal world, or is intentional about tuning in to their internal world? In what ways do you avoid, distract, or simply stay out of touch with your internal world?

2. Take some time to process the truth activity outlined in this chapter. First ask yourself: When are you most vulnerable to the lies of the enemy? When you're stressed? Tired? Hungry? Feeling isolated and alone?

3. Second: What lies does Satan tell you? Narrow it down: If the enemy could take you down with one lie, what would it be?

4. Third: Where did this lie come from? When did it begin? Is a specific experience attached to this lie? What traumas, stressors, and experiences have led you to entertaining this lie and allowing it to

become a part of your life? How does this lie impact your beliefs as well as the stories you tell yourself?

5. Lastly: How can you begin to trust God's truth over your trauma? How can you fight the lies with the truth of God's Word? Write out some specific verses that directly talk back to the lies you tend to believe. Consider writing them on note cards and placing them where you'll see them throughout the day in your attempt to replace trauma with truth.

Chapter 19

TRIGGER WARNING

Feelings Are a Signal

I LOVE THE BEACH. IT'S ONE OF MY FAVORITE PLACES IN the world. Nothing is more awe-inspiring for me than looking out at the vast, bluish-green ocean, listening to the rhythmic white noise of the waves as they crash in and then go back out, feeling the cool breeze on my face and the warm sand at my toes, smelling the salt water in the air and even tasting it as I breathe in and out. It's a full sensory experience.

Not only do I love being at the ocean, but I also love to people watch. It's always fascinating to see how people experience the beach in different ways. You've got the loungers, who often arrive at the beach bright and early with a big beach cart in tow. They meticulously lay out their blankets and chairs, getting out a good book and a drink that they put somewhere within arm's reach, and then they just lie there, soaking in the sun and hardly moving a muscle for the next six hours. Then you've got the exercise fanatics. They usually carry all their things to the beach because that is a workout in and of itself. They get out their one beach chair, which they will hardly use, and set it up just to mark their territory. Then they start their exercise routine with stretching, a few sit-ups, and a couple push-ups before hitting the sand for their five-mile run and their ocean laps. Then you've got the parents of small children, like my husband John and me. We'll bring our gear using *both* the beach cart *and* every arm and shoulder we've got because it won't fit otherwise. We lug the sand toys and shovels, six beach chairs, six towels, a cooler with drinks, the picnic lunch, the boogie boards, sunscreen (both lotion and spray), two umbrellas, a beach blanket, and a partridge in a pear tree.

And, of course, you can't forget the four kids. It's an entire ordeal. When the kids were younger, we'd pack all that plus a baby pool to keep the infant contained, a baby tent for nap time, baby food, and a few extra diapers and wipes. Now we lay it all out and then spend the next six hours hardly sitting on aforementioned chairs and blankets under the umbrella because we're chasing aforementioned children, making sand castles, getting sand out of their eyes and mouths every so often, jumping waves together, burying each other in the sand, catching crabs, hunting for seashells, applying and then reapplying sunscreen, and remaining on relatively high alert the entire time just so no one gets lost or drowns. Parents, you know what I'm talking about. To the rest of you who are exhausted just reading about it, I promise it's way more fun than it sounds.

There's another type of beachgoer who fascinates me: the treasure hunter. If you're paying attention, you'll spot a few of them on every beach. They don't camp out in just one spot, because they're usually walking mile after mile with their waterproof metal detector strapped to their arm, slowly moving to the left and back to the right as they walk. They typically have headphones on and are looking down, focused on one thing and one thing alone: finding something valuable. The last time we were at the beach, I met an older gentleman who was treasure hunting with his metal detector, and I stopped to ask him about it. He told me he had just gotten into the hobby a few months prior, and that it was addictive. He showed me how the detector worked, and the sound it made when it found something beneath the surface of the sand. He talked to me about some of the valuable things he'd found, as well as some of the false alarms.

I'm so fascinated by this process that I asked for a metal detector for my birthday, and I got one from my sweet mother-in-love. You only live once, right? Might as well look for treasure!

TUNE IN TO THE SIGNALS

I may be fascinated by these beach treasure hunters because their metal detectors remind me of the world I live in as a counselor: the world of emotions. (I can't wait to use my metal detector this summer because it's going to make for some really good counseling illustrations! Treasure hunters, stay tuned on Instagram!) Like a metal detector, emotions are the signal our body transmits as it's assessing what's going on underneath the surface of our lives. They bring our attention to the buried things we need to stop and pay attention to or deal with. We need to listen to each signal so we can respond accordingly and understand that sometimes the signal is a false alarm. Just because we hear the signal, doesn't mean we've found gold. It just means that there's something below the surface that we need to pay attention to.

I always remind my clients that emotions are real, but they aren't always true. For example, you might be feeling afraid at the thought of giving a presentation in front of your colleagues. Fear tells your body to stop, proceed with caution, and protect yourself from danger. But are you *really* in danger? Your fear response could be informed by the fact that you were picked on by your peers as a child. Your body stores all those memories and experiences, all that emotional information, in the part of your brain called the amygdala. The amygdala then uses that data, even old data from your past, to help keep you safe and secure. A significant part of having a healthy soul is being able to tune in to the signals, to recognize the real alarms *and* the false alarms, and to respond to them accordingly.

Unfortunately, many people grow up doing the exact opposite: They ignore their feelings completely. Somewhere along the way, they were taught that emotions are just a hindrance or a burden. Rather than seeing emotions as signals, they see them as weaknesses that will distract and deter them from their destination. Many Christians fall into this category when they believe "faith over feelings" means they should ignore their feelings altogether. They choose to bypass their feelings and rely only on their spirituality or their logic instead. But that concept is neither healthy, nor biblical. In fact, those who live this way are actually ignoring their God-given signals instead of responding to them.

Emotions
are real, but
they aren't
always true.

JESUS WAS EMOTIONAL

The healthiest person to walk the face of this earth was a man in tune to His emotions. We think of Jesus as so many things, but we often fail to see Him as emotional. Jesus was so aware of how He felt. When I teach this concept, I refer to the over 39 different emotions identified that Jesus experienced and expressed during His time on the earth.[1] And that's only what we know through Scripture! The Bible says that if everything Jesus did was recorded, "even the whole world would not have room for the books that would be written" (John 21:25).

Jesus allowed Himself to feel the signals His body transmitted. He modeled to us what it looks like to feel, and in doing so, gave us permission to be in tune with our own feelings.

Jesus felt joy (John 15:10-11).

Jesus felt sorrow (Luke 19:41).

Jesus felt grief (John 11:35).

Jesus felt exhaustion (John 4:6).

Jesus felt anger (Matthew 23:33).

Jesus felt compassion (Matthew 9:36).

Jesus felt agony (Luke 22:44).

Jesus felt all His feelings and then *responded* to them in a way that honored both God and the people around Him.

REACTING VERSUS RESPONDING

When Jesus felt something, He recognized the signal and then responded accordingly. To *respond* to an emotion means recognizing the feeling, getting to the bottom of what it might mean, and then choosing to act in a way that is beneficial to yourself and those around you. The opposite of responding to an emotion is *reacting* to an emotion. Reacting means instantly acting in a potentially unbeneficial way the moment you feel an emotion, rather than trying to understand it. Reacting could look like a number of different things: shutting down or withdrawing when you feel frustrated, shouting or cursing when you get angry, isolating when you feel anxious, or defaulting to an addiction to numb any uncomfortable feelings. Instead of using the feelings to help you heal, you use the feeling as an excuse for unhealthy behaviors. Remember, feelings are not bad or good; they are simply signals. It's how we respond to feelings that leads us down healthy or unhealthy paths.

Jesus responded to His sorrow with gratitude to God the Father (John 11:40-41).

Jesus responded to His exhaustion by setting limits (Luke 5:16).

Jesus responded to His anger by pursuing justice (John 2:13-22).

Jesus responded to His compassion by practically meeting the needs of those around Him (Matthew 14:13-21).

Jesus responded to His agony by going straight to the Father, by actively choosing truth in response to the pain His body was experiencing: "Being in anguish, he prayed more earnestly, and his sweat was like drops of blood falling to the ground" (Luke 22:44).

> Remember, feelings are not bad or good; they are simply signals. It's how we respond to feelings that leads us down healthy or unhealthy paths.

He didn't just feel; He responded to His feelings in a healthy way. There's so much more I could say about the emotions of Jesus.[2] But for now, I want you to consider this: How often do you react to your feelings instead of responding to them? When those big feelings come up in your life, what do you do with them? Do you just follow them wherever they lead, or do you stop to consider what they mean and how they can inform you?

TRIGGER WARNING

Something I find myself talking about often as a counselor is triggers. Triggers are those things that cause an overwhelming or exaggerated negative emotional response inside of you. They're things that set you off. It could be something you hear, or read, or see, or even smell. Something someone says or does could trigger you. Triggers can happen anywhere, anytime. The part of your brain we talked about earlier—the amygdala, which is responsible for your emotional memories—remembers things from your past and can often send out a loud alarm through an exaggerated emotional response. The purpose of the alarm is to get your attention and instigate a response—but often, what we do instead is react. We feel triggered by something someone says, so we get into a big fight and then cut them out of our lives. We're triggered by something our pastor says, so we stop attending church. We're triggered by something we see, hear, or smell, so we stop going to the places that trigger us.

The truth is, we live in an extremely trigger-avoidant culture that tells us to do whatever it takes to avoid those difficult feelings. Instead of trying to understand our triggers and get to the root of our exaggerated emotional responses, we're encouraged to just prevent them from happening ever again. Cut that person out of your life. Throw that book in the trash. Don't step back into that church. Cancel it. Delete it. Block it.

> Triggers can be gifts to us, as they invite us into the journey of healing on a deeper level.

But what if triggers are signals too? What if triggers are signs? What if the very things that trigger us are the body's way of revealing the things inside of us that need to be healed, paid attention to, and dealt with? Triggers can be gifts to us, as they invite us into the journey of healing on a deeper level. They provide opportunities to address trauma that needs to be unpacked, wounds that need to be tended to, habits that need to be changed, and relationships that need to be transformed. They're reminders that God is, in fact, still working on our souls. Your triggers are an invitation. An invitation to tune in. To acknowledge. To unpack. To heal. And to respond. My friends, each and every one of your emotions is a sheer gift. Even when it's a difficult emotion. Because emotions are God-given signals to help you pay attention to the things going on beneath the surface of your life. They convey important messages that we need to hear and acknowledge. They're spotlights shining a light on the stress that needs to be addressed, the limits that need to be set, the healing that needs to take place, and the boundaries that need to be adjusted. As we care for our souls, it's our job and our job alone to tune in to the signals and respond accordingly.[3]

Verse for Reflection

Being in anguish, he prayed more earnestly,
and his sweat was like drops of blood falling to the ground (Luke 22:44).

Today's Rhythm: FEELINGS ARE A SIGNAL

1. Do you have a positive or negative reaction to being an emotional person who is in tune with their feelings? Why do you think you react this way?

2. List three difficult emotions you've experienced this week. Then think through what those emotions may have been signaling to your body. For example: *Irritability may be my body signaling I need to get more rest and set more boundaries. Anxiety may be my body signaling that I have too much on my plate. Feeling hurt and offended may be my body signaling that I need to discuss my needs with my spouse. Sorrow may be my body signaling that I need to take some time to process my grief.*

3. Identify one trigger—something that elicits a strong emotional reaction or an exaggerated response—that tends to come up on a regular basis. What might your body be signaling to you that needs to be healed, addressed, or dealt with?

4. Do you tend to *react* to your feelings or *respond* to your feelings? List the ways you tend to react, as well as how you can begin to respond instead.

Chapter 20

SOUL CARE

Triage Your Soul

I *HATE* EMERGENCY ROOMS.

I'll do anything possible to avoid having to visit one. Not only does visiting an emergency room mean something is most likely seriously wrong with myself or someone in my family (which is why most people hate them as well), but also, the horrifically long wait adds salt to the wound! Since efficiency and time management is my love language (Dr. Gary Chapman must have forgotten to add that one to his book *The 5 Love Languages!*), I can't bear the thought of sitting in a waiting room for five hours, just to get an "urgent" appointment. It doesn't feel so urgent after five hours, does it? We've had to visit the ER a few times in the past decade—once because of some blood work that signaled I may have had an unexpected blood clot. (After a five-hour wait and a three-hour exam, I was cleared. Praise the Lord, it was a false alarm.) Another time we found ourselves in the ER in the middle of the night when our toddler had difficulty breathing. (Five hours in the waiting room and one steroid shot later, he was back home safe and sound!)

As much as I dislike the experience of the ER, I'm truly thankful for every single doctor and nurse who works tirelessly to help us feel better. We're lucky to live in a country where we have access to medical care at all hours of the day and night, even if it takes six hours. It's a gift to have a medical team ready to assess your situation, who can help you get to the bottom of what's hurting the most. Those in the medical field call this *triage*: the process of assessing the severity of your situation so they have a clear understanding of what needs immediate treatment and what can wait. If you come into the ER with a headache and hemorrhaging, they'll start with the hemorrhaging! If you walk in with a broken bone and difficulty breathing, they'll start with the breathing! They will always prioritize the issue that's most severe and life-threatening. The triage process helps medical experts focus on urgent matters and not be distracted by details. It's a decision-making process that literally saves lives.

TRIAGE YOUR SOUL

I want you to consider the process of caring for your soul in a similar way. Remember the question I asked you at the very beginning of this book? I want to ask it one more time: How full do you feel? By now, I expect you've really considered your answer. But this time, I want to ask you a follow-up question: Which of the six rhythms of soul care that we've discussed throughout this book is in the most need? Let's do a triage of your soul. Let's take a moment to review the six areas we learned about:

1. **NOURISH**: Caring for your soul through nutrition, hydration, and movement.

2. **REST**: Caring for your soul through rhythms of rest and a sustainable pace of life.

3. **CONNECT**: Caring for your soul through life-giving relationships.

4. **PROTECT**: Caring for your soul with boundaries that protect your calling.

5. **SAVOR:** Caring for your soul by being present, practicing gratitude, and intentionally enjoying life.

6. **TUNE IN:** Caring for your soul by having insight and understanding of your inner world.

Take some time to think through each of these areas and ask God to reveal to you where you need to begin. Which area is in most need of attention and care? Which area is most severely impacting the health of your soul? This triage is really important, because if you try to implement all of the above right away, you'll get overwhelmed. It won't be long until you're feeling burned-out from trying not to be burned-out. You must pace yourself in this process. For lasting change to occur, you first have to narrow down the area in most need of care and start there.

START WITH WHAT'S MOST SEVERE

As you're pondering where to begin, think in terms of severity. Ask yourself this: *Which of these rhythms is most significantly missing from my life?* When you consider the times you find yourself feeling the most stressed, the most depleted, and the most burned-out, which one of the above rhythms is typically out of sync? Is your physical body being neglected? Is it a lack of sleep? Is it a lack of boundaries and feeling spread too thin? Are you feeling lonely and isolated? Is life devoid of fun and joy? Are your emotions overwhelming in a way you don't know how to manage? If you're still having a hard time figuring out where to begin, I've created a short assessment you can take to help you narrow down which of the soul care rhythms you are most in need of practicing. You can find this free quiz at DebraFileta.com/soulcarequiz.

GET TO THE ROOT

At the beginning of this book, I talked to you about the importance of getting to the *why*. *Why* does this area tend to be a struggle for you? Why do you neglect your body, fail to rest, struggle with boundaries, withdraw and isolate, forget to have fun, or live with little to no insight into your internal world? What lies or false beliefs tend to perpetuate this cycle in your life? What beliefs did you learn from your childhood, or through other life experiences, that have fueled your lack of soul care? Before we begin to "treat" the symptoms of the problem, we have to find the root of what caused the original problem. What has perpetuated a lack of soul care in this area of your life, and where did it begin? What false beliefs have been holding you back from caring for yourself, and from living filled in the way God has called you to live? Each soul care rhythm may even come with a different reason as to why it's been a neglected part of your life. Maybe you've failed to nourish your body because you believed the lie that your spirit is the only thing that matters. Maybe you've failed to rest because you believe God only loves you when you're *doing* for Him rather than just *being*. Maybe you've failed to set boundaries and protect yourself because you believed the lie that boundaries are unnecessary or harmful, and that Christians should always say yes.

Maybe you've lived in isolation and lack of community because you believed the lie that you are not worth loving. Maybe you've never savored life because you believed you don't deserve to have joy because of the mistakes you've made. Maybe you've failed to have insight and understanding with what's going on underneath the surface of your life because you believed the lie that emotions are weak, wrong, or meaningless. You must get to the root of *why*. Why have you struggled in this area? How can you begin to shift your beliefs and align them with God's truth? What truths can take the place of those lies and allow you to live a life of soul care? You deserve a life that is filled to the brim and overflowing into the lives of those around you.

SOUL CARE PLAN

Once you've narrowed down the soul care rhythm you need to begin with and gotten to the roots of *why* it's been neglected, I challenge you to go back to that specific section and reread it with fresh eyes. Reread it with the goal of coming up with a soul care plan. Map out what you want to change, and how you're going to change it. In my book *Reset*, I talk about the importance of understanding the five stages of change: precontempla-tion (deciding whether you're ready for a change), contemplation (finding more pros to changing than staying the same), preparation (coming up with your plan to change), action (putting your plan into practice), and maintenance (when the process of change becomes your new way of life).[1] After you've identified the soul care rhythm that needs to change and why you need to change it, you'll need an actual plan to change it.

Once you've chosen where to begin, make a list of practical first steps to take to begin caring for your soul in this way. Remember, if you really want something to last, you have to keep it simple. Simplicity is easier to sustain in the long term.

Consider making a copy of the following template to guide you as you map out your soul care plan. Once you've mastered this specific rhythm, you can use this template to guide you through the other rhythms as well.

SOUL CARE PLAN

Today's Date: _____

Which rhythm am I most in need of practicing? Circle one of the following:

NOURISH   REST   CONNECT   PROTECT   SAVOR   TUNE IN

On a scale of zero to ten (ten being the *most care* and zero being the *least care*), give yourself a number to represent how well you have cared for this area of your life: _____

Write out three ways you tend to neglect or overlook this area of your life. *I tend to neglect this area of my life by...*

1. _____
2. _____
3. _____

What are some signs and symptoms that this area is in need of care?

1. _____
2. _____
3. _____

What underlying lie or belief fuels this particular problem in your life (the *why*)?

Write out the underlying false belief that you have about God, others, or self that tends to hold you back from practicing this rhythm in your life. *I falsely believe that...*

What truth can you adopt to begin replacing this lie? *I choose to believe that...*

Write out five ways you will begin practicing soul care in this area of your life. *I will practice this rhythm and care for my soul by...*

1. _____

2. _____

3. _____

4. _____

5. _____

Choose someone with whom you will share your plan and who can help you stay on track as you care for your soul. Write down the name of one person you will invite into your soul care journey:

_____

Come back to your soul care plan often to refresh and review. Three months from now, rate yourself one more time to assess how you are doing in this specific rhythm of soul care.

Three Month Assessment: On a scale of zero to ten (ten being the *most care* and zero being the *least care*), give yourself a rating to represent how well you have cared for this area of your life in the past three months: _____

THE HEALTH OF YOUR SOUL

Do you know why all of this matters so incredibly much? Because the health of your soul isn't just for you. It's also for everyone you care about, interact with, and influence. Your life is entangled with the lives of so many others. Whether you want it to be, and whether you even believe it, the health of your soul directly impacts everyone God has placed into your life. It impacts your spouse, your children, your family, your friends, your coworkers, your community, and your brothers and sisters in Christ. When you neglect yourself, you are neglecting an important part of the fully functioning body of Christ.

> The health of your soul directly impacts everyone God has placed into your life.

God's Word refers to Christians using the analogy of the body. First Corinthians 12:12 says, "There is one body, but it has many parts. But all its many parts make up one body" (NIrv). You are divinely interconnected with a community of believers. No matter how you view yourself, and whether or not you believe you have an important role in the body of Christ, you are absolutely necessary. "The eye can't say to the hand, 'I don't need you!' The head can't say to the feet, 'I don't need you!' In fact, it is just the opposite. The parts of the body that seem to be weaker are the ones we can't do without" (1 Corinthians 12:21-22 NIrv). No matter what role you have, you are an integral part of the functioning of the body of Christ. Though it may not always *feel* significant, your portion has a great impact on all the rest. And not only that, but your role and impact has been divinely placed: "God has placed each part in the body just as he wanted it to be" (1 Corinthians 12:18 NIrv). When you neglect the caring of your soul, your portion of the body begins to break down—and its failure has a significant and often devastating impact on the rest of the body. Your job is to care for your portion of the body so it can continue operating smoothly and have a positive impact on every other part.

I witnessed a devastating case recently, involving a senior pastor who had an affair with a woman from his congregation. As a licensed counselor,

I often have the grave responsibility of sitting with pastors or high-impact leaders as they begin to pick up the remnants of a life that shattered under burdens they were never meant to carry. Some men and women have lived empty for so long that it all finally catches up to them. And while there are so many things to sift through, one theme that comes up again and again in these situations is an utter neglect of soul care—so much time spent caring for the souls of everyone else, and so little time caring for and protecting their own souls. Maybe we believe we're invincible, and we assume it will never happen to us. Maybe, because we're Christians, we falsely believe that our spirituality somehow makes us immune to the burnout. No matter the answer, I find the most devastating portion of these stories is the ripple effect they have on the rest of the body. The spouse, the children, the family, the church, the community. And the lesson at the end of the brokenness and pain always goes something like this: "If I only knew how important caring for my soul was, and how many people my emptiness would impact, I would have considered soul care the most selfless thing I could've done for my family." When we neglect our portion of the body, it impacts all the rest.

What if caring for your own soul really is a selfless act? In taking care of your portion of the body, you are allowing and enabling the other parts to fully function in the ways God intended. Your job is to continue to take inventory—to triage and care for your own soul—so you can be available for those to whom God has divinely connected you. "In that way, the parts of the body will not take sides. All of them will take care of one another. If one part suffers, every part suffers with it. If one part is honored, every part shares in its joy" (1 Corinthians 12:25-26 NIrv). It's never too late to heal the portion that's been entrusted to you. It's never too late to begin caring for your soul.

> What if caring for your own soul really is a selfless act?

BURNING OUT OR SHINING BRIGHT

I believe the enemy wants to completely deplete us and make us as ineffective as possible. He wants to empty us so we're tired, irritable, lacking in joy, filled with anxiety and stress, and doing the bare minimum just to survive. He wants us thoroughly burned-out. He wants to snuff out our God-given light, or at least dim it to the point that it's no longer a threat to him. It reminds me of that song we sang in Sunday school that we all know so well: "This little light of mine, I'm gonna let it shine…let it shine, let it shine, let it shine." But the real mantra came toward the end of the song, when we all proclaimed, "Won't let Satan *pfffff* it out—I'm gonna let it shine…" And with that, we declared we would never let Satan blow out our light!

Looking back, I don't think any of us really grasped what that song meant as little second graders singing at the top of our lungs. I know I certainly didn't. I didn't yet understand all the stressors of life and the many demands that were coming my way—the responsibility of getting an education and making a living, the hard work of creating a healthy marriage, raising children, and keeping a house running. The demands of family, friends, and ministry. The busy schedules and calendars and obligations. The curveballs of health issues and financial stressors and mental health struggles and unexpected trauma and tragedy and grief and loss. You don't really think anything will blow out your little light…until one day it does. One day, you stop and realize you've been living with just a flicker at best. Or maybe, just maybe, your little light is completely dead and gone.

> There is a battle going on for the health of your soul. And soul care is how you fight back.

I truly believe there is a battle going on for the health of your soul. And soul care is how you fight back. Soul care is how you fill up and prepare yourself for battle. Soul care is how you invite the power, presence, and practices of Jesus to give you what you need—just as the Father gave Jesus exactly what He needed during His time here on earth. Soul care is how we remain filled, so we can live fully. Soul care is how we replenish, so we can continue to pour out. Soul care is how we tend to our little light so it keeps shining, and shining brightly.

I guess you could say that the opposite of burning out is shining bright. And you can't shine bright unless you are fueling yourself with the rhythms and practices that will keep your flame alive. Tend to your flame and keep it shining bright. "You are the light of the world...Let your light shine before others, that they may see your good deeds and glorify your Father in heaven" (Matthew 5:14, 16).

My prayer for each of you who has reached the end of this book is for your eyes to remain opened to the importance of caring for and tending to your soul. I am praying for you, first and foremost, that you would know what it means to have a meaningful relationship with Jesus, the lover of your soul. Second, I pray you would commit to practicing the rhythms of nourish, rest, connect, protect, savor, and tune in on a regular basis, so you can remain healthy, filled, and effective. Because the opposite of living empty is living filled. And the opposite of burning out is shining bright. It's time to let your little light shine. It's time to care for the health of your soul. It's time to *live filled* so you can *live fully*. "I pray that you, being rooted and established in love...*may be filled to the measure of all the fullness of God*. Now to him who is able to do immeasurably more than all we ask or imagine, according to his power that is at work within us, to him be glory in the church and in Christ Jesus throughout all generations, for ever and ever! Amen" (Ephesians 3:17, 19-21, emphasis mine). It's time for us to live filled, in Jesus's name.

Verses for Reflection

I pray that you, being rooted and established in love...
may be filled to the measure of all the fullness of God (Ephesians 3:17, 19).

Today's Rhythm: TRIAGE YOUR SOUL

1. "What if caring for your own soul really is a selfless act?" Reflect on that quote from today's chapter, then journal your thoughts, reactions, and feelings about this question.

2. Do a soul triage: Make a copy of the soul care plan (pp. 196-197). Which rhythm of caring for your soul has been the most neglected and is in most need of care?

3. In what ways has neglecting this specific area of your life impacted both you and the people around you?

4. Take some time today to think through and fill out the soul care plan. Consider where you need to begin, and choose practical steps you can take to begin implementing this specific rhythm in your life.

SOUL SEARCHING

Before you can begin caring for your soul, you've got to know the One who created your soul! This entire book is focused on the rhythms and practices of Jesus, because He is the only One who truly knows our souls. The Bible says He alone can restore and refresh our souls (Psalm 23:3). If you've never made the decision to begin a relationship with Jesus, I encourage you to start here. He loves you and cares for every part of your life more than you could even imagine.

PRAY WITH ME:

Jesus, I thank You that You love me enough to open my eyes to truth. I recognize that I can't fully know who I am until I know You. I can't fully care for my soul until I know the One who created my soul. You're the only One who can truly fill me up. Today, I affirm that I want to be in a relationship with You. I believe that You died on the cross to take away my sins, I believe You rose from the dead to make a way for me to be with You for eternity. I want to live for You today and always. I want to see myself through Your eyes. Fill me with Your Spirit and give me the grace I need to live for You each day. I want to shine brightly for You. In the name of Jesus, amen.

If you prayed this prayer for the first time in your life, I want you to know that I am overjoyed! In fact, I want to hear from you. Email me at connect@debrafileta.com, and let me help you take the next steps on your journey with Jesus—the true lover of your soul!

APPENDIX A

Identifying and Treating Mental Health Struggles

MENTAL ILLNESS DOESN'T REFLECT A *CHARACTER* ISSUE; it reflects a *chemistry* issue. Mental illness is caused by changes in the functioning of neurochemicals in the brain (primarily serotonin and dopamine), which begin to impact the rest of the body. Just like we would prescribe insulin and lifestyle changes for a person with diabetes, we must also understand the role of proper medication and counseling for a person who is struggling with a mental health disorder. A mental health struggle is not a reflection of a person's strength or faith, and it's important to reiterate that to the struggling individual. There is hope for healing!

Depression and anxiety are two of the most commonly reported mental health struggles permeating the church at large. It's important to have a healthy understanding of how they present. Feeling worry is not the same as generalized anxiety. Feeling sad is not the same as major depressive disorder. It's not the feeling that defines the struggle; it's the presenting symptoms. If you have been feeling stuck for a significant amount of time, it's important to consider whether an undiagnosed and untreated mental health struggle may be holding you back. Here is a list of symptoms to consider. Please consult with a medical doctor or a licensed professional counselor if you exhibit any of the following:

TABLE 1: Major Depressive Disorder (MDD)

This is a common yet serious mood disorder that impacts a person's daily life. It's also referred to as clinical depression. This disorder is above and beyond the feeling of sadness; it permeates many parts of the individual's life.

It can be diagnosed when a person exhibits five or more of the following symptoms in a two-week period:

- Depressed mood (most days, most of the day), including sadness, emptiness, hopelessness (may present as tearful)
- Loss of interest or pleasure (may present as a lack of excitement, joy, interest in relationships, etc.)
- Weight loss or gain and decrease or increase in appetite
- Insomnia or hypersomnia (not sleeping well or sleeping too much)
- Psychomotor retardation or agitation (slowed movements)
- Fatigue or a lack of energy
- Feelings of worthlessness or excessive guilt
- Decreased concentration
- Thoughts of suicide or death

It's important to understand that it may be a depressive disorder if these symptoms negatively impact other areas of the person's life, including one's job, social life, relationships, etc., and if the symptoms are not related to another medical condition or medication.

TABLE 2: Generalized Anxiety Disorder (GAD)

- The presence of excessive worry for a period of six months or more

- The worry is experienced as very difficult to control, and may move from one topic to another over time

- The anxiety and worry are also accompanied by physical symptoms (in adults *three* of the following symptoms, and in children only *one* of the following is necessary for a diagnosis):

  - Edginess or restlessness

  - Fatigue or consistent lack of energy

  - Difficulty concentrating

  - Irritability

  - Increased muscle aches or soreness

  - Difficulty sleeping (trouble falling asleep, staying asleep, restlessness at night, or unsatisfying sleep)

The worry and anxiety displayed can revolve around a number of things, including health concerns for self or others, job responsibilities, financial concerns, or everyday life matters. It's often accompanied by a need to seek reassurance from others.

Please note that sometimes generalized anxiety can be accompanied by panic attacks. Because panic attacks often present as physical symptoms, they can be hard to identify and are often confused with a medical condition.

TABLE 3: Panic Attacks/Disorder

- Chest pain or discomfort

- Shortness of breath

- Hot flashes or chills

- Excessive sweating

- Feeling of choking

- Fear of dying

- Fear of losing control or "going crazy"
- Feeling dizzy, faint, or lightheaded
- Accelerated heart rate or palpitations
- Nausea or abdominal stress
- Numbness or tingling sensations
- Feelings of unreality or being detached from oneself (called depersonalization)
- Trembling or shaking

Symptoms of a panic attack usually happen suddenly, lasting about ten minutes before subsiding. Some attacks may last longer or happen in succession. Panic disorder also causes the fear or worry that the episode may happen again. This sometimes causes the individual to avoid certain situations for fear of an episode.

HOW TO TREAT MENTAL ILLNESS

The following treatment methods are most effective in battling depression and anxiety:

Therapy

Therapy is a profound experience. Unlike anything else, the process guides you through the difficult emotions and hard experiences in a hope-filled way. It helps you counter faulty thinking, gives you skills to process difficult past experiences, and offers renewed perspective and hope for the future. Not only that, but it's proven to be effective as a primary treatment method for people struggling with mental illness. In fact, it can be just as effective as medication when it comes to treating mild to moderate mental illness.

Online options now make it more convenient than ever to enter therapy, offering an easier route for those who might be reluctant to go see a therapist in person. If you do not have a trusted therapist or need a guide to find a good therapist, visit DebraFileta.com/resources.

Medication

Medication is a recommended treatment method for people struggling with moderate to severe symptoms of anxiety and depression. The role of these medications (commonly known as antidepressants or SSRIs) is to increase the neurochemicals in the body that are responsible for regulating mood. Not only can they be beneficial to someone who is struggling, but they can also be life-changing. These medications can be prescribed by a medical doctor. If you've been feeling stuck for a significant amount of time, I challenge you to get a clinical assessment with a medical doctor or licensed counselor to rule out any underlying mental health struggles.

APPENDIX B

How to Find a Counselor

FINDING A GOOD COUNSELOR CAN SEEM LIKE A DAUNT-
ing process for many people. In fact, it's one of the most common questions I receive. To get you started with this process, I put together a brief checklist:

1. **The most common route to finding a counselor (or pretty much anything these days) is by doing an internet search.** You want to make sure you are searching for a Christian licensed counselor. Many people who use the term *counselor* may be pastorally certified but not licensed by the state. The term *licensed* means they are trained professionals who have undergone a specific amount of training and education.

2. **Usually, a counselor's biography will list some of their areas of specialty, such as sex therapy, trauma, depression and anxiety, addictions, etc.** Try to connect with a counselor who serves your specific area of struggle. Feel free to give them a call or send an email before scheduling your first session. Ask them what type of therapy they typically use,

how many years they've been in practice, as well as how they integrate the Christian faith into their clinical approach.

3. **Remember that when it comes to a good counselor, it's all about finding someone you feel comfortable with.** The therapeutic relationship between you and your counselor is important, but it's not uncommon not to hit it off right away. I always recommend trying between three and six sessions with a counselor before you attempt to find another one. If you don't feel the connection or don't feel comfortable after a handful of sessions, please don't quit! Just find another counselor and try again. There's no offense taken if you don't connect; the only true offense is if you give up on your situation! Reach out to another counselor—and in some cases, even another *and* another—and try again.

4. **Always remember that healing is not linear; it's cyclical.** What I mean is, you don't just get better and better each day. Sometimes you'll take a few steps forward and one step back. Sometimes you'll struggle. Sometimes you'll want to give up. But the key is to continue moving forward, because as you do, you'll grow healthier and stronger and move closer to your goals. Healing is not only possible, but also *attainable* for those who are willing to put in the work.

5. **You can reach out to us for counseling options and resources.** For the opportunity of connecting with me or one of the Christian counselors from my team, find us at DebraFileta.com/counseling.

Notes

Chapter Two: Self-Care Versus Soul Care

1. Rick Warren, *The Purpose Driven Life* (Nashville, TN: Zondervan, 2012), 149.

Chapter Three: Don't Push Through

1. It's important to differentiate signs and symptoms of burnout from those of clinical depression. See Appendix A for more on how to differentiate.

Chapter Four: Don't Self-Destruct

1. To learn more about the timeline activity, see pages 28–30 in *Are You Really OK?*, by Debra Fileta (Eugene, OR: Harvest House Publishers, 2021).

2. Allow us to help you on your journey of healing by booking a session with one of the Christian counselors on my team at the Debra Fileta Counselors Network. See Debra Fileta.com/counseling.

Chapter Five: Empty Things Can't Fill Empty People

1. Mohammad Yaqub, "20+ Fascinating Coffee Spending Statistics," BusinessDIT, https://www.businessdit.com/coffee-spending-statistics.

2. Mansoor Iqbal, "Netflix Revenue and Usage Statistics," Business of Apps, https://www.businessofapps.com/data/netflix-statistics.

3. Lyndon Azcuna, "The Porn Pandemic," Life Plan, https://www.lifeplan.org/the-porn-pandemic.

4. Jack Flynn, "25+ Amazon Statistics [2023]: Facts About the Largest U.S. E-Commerce Market," https://www.zippia.com/advice/amazon-statistics.

5. Simon Kemp, "Digital 2023 Deep-Dive: How Much Time Do We Spend on Social Media?," Datareportal, https://datareportal.com/reports/digital-2023-deep-dive-time-spent-on-social-media.

6. Lyndon Azcuna, "The Porn Pandemic," Life Plan, https://www.lifeplan.org/the-porn-pandemic.

7. Shari Mason, "40+ Shocking Fast Food Statistics For 2023," https://eatpallet.com/fast-food-statistics.

8. Kevin Wheeler, "A 'Dry January' is good for more than just a healthy liver. Here's what else will improve if you stop drinking.," *USA Today*, January 9, 2020, https://www.usatoday.com/story/money/2020/01/08/dry-january-could-save-millennials-more-money-than-they-think/2831655001.

9. Ash Turner, "Average Screen Time: iPhone and Android Statistics (Sep 2023 Update)," Bank My Cell, https://www.bankmycell.com/blog/average-screen-time-on-iphone-android.

Chapter Six: Come and Eat

1. David Sharp, "An 87-year-old woman fought off an 'awfully hungry' home intruder and then fed him," *National Post*, August 3, 2023, https://nationalpost.com/news/an-87-year-old-woman-fought-off-an-intruder-then-fed-him-after-he-told-her-he-was-awfully-hungry.

2. Nicole Spector, "The science behind being 'hangry,'" NBC News BETTER, July 2, 2018, https://www.nbcnews.com/better/pop-culture/science-behind-being-hangry-ncna887806.

3. Don Colbert, *What Would Jesus Eat?* (Nashville, TN: Thomas Nelson, 2002), xiv.

4. Marian L. Neuhouser, "The Importance of Healthy Dietary Patterns in Chronic Disease Prevention," *Nutrition Research*, Vol. 70 (October 2019): 3–6, https://doi.org/10.1016/j.nutres.2018.06.002.

5. Two books regarding nutrition that you should add to your reading list are *What Would Jesus Eat?* and *The Maker's Diet*.

Chapter Seven: It Might Not Be a Demon

1. Levi Lusko, foreword to *Are You Really OK?*, by Debra Fileta (Eugene, OR: Harvest House Publishers, 2021), 10.

2. Sue J. Nelson, "The Fascinating Symbolism of Water in the Bible: 9 Attributes," Women of Noble Character, https://www.womanofnoblecharacter.com/water-in-the-bible.

3. W.H. Auden, *The Complete Works of W.H. Auden*, Prose: Volume III: 1949–1955 (Princeton, NJ: Princeton University Press, 2008), 482.

4. Molly Sargen, "Biological Roles of Water: Why is water necessary for life?", Harvard University, Graduate School of Arts and Sciences, https://sitn.hms.harvard.edu/uncategorized/2019/biological-roles-of-water-why-is-water-necessary-for-life.

5. "Water and Healthier Drinks," Center for Disease Control and Prevention, https://www.cdc.gov/healthyweight/healthy_eating/water-and-healthier-drinks.html.

6. Ana Adan, "Cognitive Performance and Dehydration," *Journal of the American College of Nutrition*, Vol. 31, no. 2 (June 2013): 71–78, https://www.tandfonline.com/doi/abs/10.1080/07315724.2012.10720011.

7. Honor Whiteman, "Drinking Water Boosts Your Brain's Reaction Time," Medical News Today, July 20, 2013, https://www.medicalnewstoday.com/articles/263648#1.

8. Lucy Soto, "Protect Your Heart and Health During the 'Dog Days' of Summer," https://www.heart.org/en/news/2018/07/20/protect-your-heart-and-health-during-the-dog-days-of-summer.

9. "Rehydration Therapy," Center for Disease Control and Prevention, https://www.cdc.gov/cholera/treatment/rehydration-therapy.html.

Chapter Eight: Walking with Jesus

1. Estera Wieja, "10 Places Where Jesus Walked in Israel from Scripture," Fellowship of Israel Related Ministries, https://firmisrael.org/learn/10-places-where-jesus-walked.

2. "Exercise: 7 Benefits of Regular Physical Activity," Mayo Clinic, https://www.mayoclinic.org/healthy-lifestyle/fitness/in-depth/exercise/art-20048389.

3. Srini Pillay, "How Simply Moving Benefits Your Mental Health," *Harvard Health* (blog), https://www.health.harvard.edu/blog/how-simply-moving-benefits-your-mental-health-201603289350.

4. Gary M. Cooney et al., "Exercise for Depression," National Library for Medicine, https://pubmed.ncbi.nlm.nih.gov/24026850/.

5. R. Robertson et al., "Walking for Depression or Depressive Symptoms: A Systematic Review and Meta-Analysis," National Library of Medicine, https://www.ncbi.nlm.nih.gov/books/NBK99429/.

6. Janice Neumann, "Regular Walking Can Help Ease Depression," *Scientific American*, January 30, 2015, https://www.scientificamerican.com/article/regular-walking-can-help-ease-depression/.

7. Simon N. Young, "How to Increase Serotonin in the Human Brain Without Drugs," *Journal of Psychiatry & Neuroscience,* Vol. 32, no. 6 (November 2007): 394-399, https://www.ncbi.nlm.nih.gov/pmc/articles/PMC2077351/.

8. Gary Thomas, "Learn Why Your Body & Health Matters," Saddleback Church, YouTube video, https://www.youtube.com/watch?v=w4DziQTEmfw.

9. Thomas, "Learn Why Your Body & Health Matters," https://www.youtube.com/watch?v=w4DziQTEmfw.

Chapter Nine: Jesus Took Naps

1. David Mathis, "Do You Sleep Less Than Jesus?" Desiring God, https://www.desiringgod.org/articles/do-you-sleep-less-than-jesus.

2. James B. Maas, "Learning about the Power of Sleep," *New York Times on the Web,* https://archive.nytimes.com/www.nytimes.com/books/first/m/maas-sleep.html?ref=driverlayer.com/web.

3. See Appendix B.

4. From *Are You Really OK?,* by Debra Fileta (Eugene, OR: Harvest House Publishers, 2021), 206–207.

Chapter Eleven: Stay Connected

1. C.S. Lewis, *The Four Loves* (New York, NY: HarperCollins, 2012), 121.

2. G. Oscar Anderson and Colette Thayer, "Loneliness and Social Connections: A National Survey of Adults 45 and Older," AARP Research, https://www.aarp.org/research/topics/life/info-2018/loneliness-social-connections.html.

3. Julianna Holt-Lunstad, Timothy B. Smith, and J. Bradley Layton, "Social Relationships and Mortality Risk: A Meta-Analytic Review," *PLOS Medicine*, https://doi.org/10.1371/journal.pmed.1000316.

4. Zara Abrams, "The Science of Why Friendships Keep Us Healthy," American Psychological Association, https://www.apa.org/monitor/2023/06/cover-story-science-friendship.

5. Julianne Holt-Lunstad et al., "Loneliness and Social Isolation as Risk Factors for Mortality: A Meta-Analytic Review," *Sage Journals*, Vol. 10, no. 2 (March 2015) https://journals.sagepub.com/doi/full/10.1177/1745691614568352.

6. Holt-Lunstad et al., "Loneliness and Social Isolation as Risk Factors for Mortality: A Meta-Analytic Review," https://journals.sagepub.com/doi/full/10.1177/1745691614568352.

7. Julianne Holt-Lunstad et al., "On the Importance of Relationship Quality: The Impact of Ambivalence in Friendships on Cardiovascular Functioning," *Annals of Behavioral Medicine*, Vol. 33, no. 3 (June 2007): 278–290, https://doi.org/10.1007/BF02879910.

8. Karmel W. Choi et al., "An Exposure-Wide and Mendelian Randomization Approach to Identifying Modifiable Factors for the Prevention of Depression," *The American Journal of Psychiatry*, Vol. 177, no. 10 (October 2020): 944-954, https://doi.org/10.1176/appi.ajp.2020.19111158.

9. Tiana Herring, "The Research is Clear: Solitary Confinement Causes Long-Lasting Harm," Prison Policy Initiative, https://www.prisonpolicy.org/blog/2020/12/08/solitary_symposium/.

10. Herring, "The Research is Clear: Solitary Confinement Causes Long-Lasting Harm."

11. Jessica Brodie, "What Every Christian Needs to Know About Koinonia," CrossWalk, https://www.crosswalk.com/faith/spiritual-life/what-every-christian-needs-to-know-about-koinonia.html.

12. Connect with our team of Christian counselors or apply to be a part of our team at DebraFileta.com/counseling.

13. Bob Goff, *Everybody Always* (Nashville, TN: Nelson Books, 2018), 5.

Chapter Thirteen: Jesus Loves Boundaries

1. Let's be Instagram friends! Connect with me @DebraFileta. I absolutely love hearing from you!

Chapter Fifteen: Enjoy Life

1. Max Lucado, *He Gets Us* (Nashville, TN: Thomas Nelson, 2023), 53–55.

Chapter Sixteen: Savor Life

1. Connect with our team of Christian counselors at DebraFileta.com/counseling.

Chapter Seventeen: Celebrate Life

1. Warren W. Wiersbe, *Old Testament: Genesis-Deuteronomy (The Pentateuch)*, The Bible Exposition Commentary Series (Colorado Springs, CO: Victor, 2001), 258.

2. Robert A. Emmons, Michael E. McCullough, "Counting Blessings Versus Burdens: An Experimental Investigation of Gratitude and Subjective Well-Being in Daily Life," *Journal of Personality and Social Psychology*, Vol 84(2) (2003): 337-389, https://doi.org/10.1037//0022-3514.84.2.377

3. Ahmad Valikhani et al., "The Relationship Between Dispositional Gratitude and Quality of Life: The Mediating Role of Perceived Stress and Mental Health," *Personality and Individual Differences*, Vol. 141 (April 2019): 40–46, https://doi.org/10.1016/j.paid.2018.12.014.

4. Ernst T. Bohlmeijer et al., "Promoting Gratitude as a Resource for Sustainable Mental Health: Results of a 3-Armed Randomized Controlled Trial up to 6 Months Follow-Up," *Journal of Happiness Studies*, Vol. 22 (May 2020): 1011–1032, https://doi.org/10.1007/s10902-020-00261-5.

Chapter Eighteen: A Person of Insight

1. See a similar analogy in one of my previous books, *Are You Really OK?* (Eugene, OR: Harvest House Publishers, 2021), 33.

2. If you are looking for a Christian counselor, please take a look at our team at the Debra Fileta Counselors Network at DebraFileta.com/counseling.

Chapter Nineteen: Trigger Warning

1. Bill Gaultiere, "How to Feel Your Emotions with Jesus," Soul Shepherding, https://www.soulshepherding.org/how-to-feel-your-emotions-with-jesus.

2. For more on the emotions of Jesus and how to understand and process your own, read Section 1: Emotional Health in *Are You Really OK?* by Debra Fileta (Eugene, OR: Harvest House Publishers, 2021).

3. If you need help recognizing and understanding your emotions, please consider working with someone from our team of Christian counselors at DebraFileta.com/counseling.

Chapter Twenty: Soul Care

1. See Debra Fileta, *Reset* (Eugene, OR: Harvest House Publishers, 2023).

Acknowledgments

I'M SO GRATEFUL FOR A PUBLISHING COMPANY THAT feels more like family. The team at Harvest House is like no other, and I am so grateful to be partnered with them in the pursuit of spreading the message of hope and healing in Jesus's name! Thank you for believing in me from the beginning, and enthusiastically coming alongside me one book after the other. I'm so excited for all that's to come!

A huge thank you to Sherrie Slopianka, a dear friend and trusted leader. You are one of a kind. Thank you for always being available and involved. To Bob Hawkins, for your gospel-focused heart for reaching the lost and for never straying from the mission and heart of Jesus. To Audrey Greeson, my newest editor and friend. You are so easy to love! Thank you for your editing skills but mostly for your heart of gold. And to everyone else on the Harvest House team, working faithfully behind the scenes: Kari Duffy, Lindsay Lewis, Sharon Shook, and too many others to name. Thank you to each one of you for your work, for your heart, and for your role in bringing this message to life. It does not go unnoticed!

Thank you to my husband, John, my four kids, and my friends and family, for always listening to my ideas and letting me flesh out the concepts of this book in real-time.

And finally, to Jesus...the Lover of my soul. This is all for You. There is no other reason. There is no other purpose. And there is no one more worthy.

About the Author

DEBRA FILETA (M.A., LPC) is a licensed professional counselor, national speaker, and author of numerous books including *Reset* and *Are You Really OK?* She's also the founder of the Debra Fileta Counselors Network. Through her popular blog (TrueLoveDates.com) and her hotline-style podcast, she shares the message that healthy people make healthy relationships. Debra and her husband, John, have been happily married for 17 years and have four amazing children. www.DebraFileta.com

Scripture Versions Used

Unless otherwise indicated, all Scripture verses are taken from the Holy Bible, New International Version®, NIV®. Copyright © 1973, 1978, 1984, 2011 by Biblica, Inc.™ Used by permission of Zondervan. All rights reserved worldwide. www.zondervan.com. The "NIV" and "New International Version" are trademarks registered in the United States Patent and Trademark Office by Biblica, Inc.™

Verses marked ESV are taken from the ESV® Bible (The Holy Bible, English Standard Version®), copyright © 2001 by Crossway, a publishing ministry of Good News Publishers. Used by permission. All rights reserved.

Verses marked NLT are taken from the Holy Bible, New Living Translation, copyright © 1996, 2004, 2015 by Tyndale House Foundation. Used by permission of Tyndale House Publishers, Inc., Carol Stream, Illinois 60188. All rights reserved

Verses marked NIrV are taken from the Holy Bible, New International Reader's Version®, NIrV®. Copyright © 1995, 1996, 1998, 2014 by Biblica, Inc.™ Used by permission of Zondervan, www.zondervan.com. The "NIrV" and "New International Reader's Version" are trademarks registered in the United States Patent and Trademark Office by Biblica, Inc.™ [November 2022]

Verses marked GNT are taken from the Good News Translation in Today's English Version–Second Edition. Copyright © 1992 by American Bible Society. Used by Permission.

Verses marked ERV are taken from the HOLY BIBLE: EASY-TO-READ VERSION © 2014 by Bible League International. Used by permission.

Verse marked MSG are taken from The Message, copyright © 1993, 2002, 2018 by Eugene H. Peterson. Used by permission of NavPress. All rights reserved. Represented by Tyndale House Publishers.

Verses marked CEV are taken from the Contemporary English Version Copyright © 1991, 1992, 1995 by American Bible Society, Used by permission.

Verses marked HCSB have been taken from the Holman Christian Standard Bible®, Used by Permission HCSB © 1999, 2000, 2002, 2003, 2009 Holman Bible Publishers. Holman Christian Standard Bible®, Holman CSB®, and HCSB® are federally registered trademarks of Holman Bible Publishers.

Verses marked NASB are taken from the (NASB®) New American Standard Bible®, Copyright © 1960, 1971, 1977, 1995, 2020 by The Lockman Foundation. Used by permission. All rights reserved. www.lockman.org.

With **Reset,** author and professional counselor Debra Fileta will guide you through 31 powerful and sustainable practices that will help you transform your life from the inside out.

FOREWORD BY LEVI LUSKO

ARE YOU REALLY

OK

?K

GETTING REAL
ABOUT WHO YOU ARE,
HOW YOU'RE DOING,
AND WHY IT MATTERS

**DEBRA
FILETA**

M.A., LPC

Pursuing the spiritual, emotional, mental, and physical health God desires for you is a lifelong commitment that requires honest self-examination and intentional living. In *Are You Really OK?* author and licensed counselor Debra Fileta will help you take inventory of yourself so you can recognize where you need growth and healing.

To learn more about Harvest House books and
to read sample chapters, visit our website:

www.HarvestHousePublishers.com

HARVEST HOUSE PUBLISHERS
EUGENE, OREGON